beazley
the **designs of the year**
DESIGN
MUSEUM

BEAZLEY DESIGNS OF THE YEAR 2017

CONTENTS

FOREWORD
Andrew Horton
Chief Executive Officer, Beazley plc

Beazley is proud to partner with the Design Museum
and to support the Beazley Designs of the Year.
As a specialist insurer we are well placed to
understand the value of good design. We
see first-hand the consequences when things
go wrong and our products and services are
expertly designed to help people and
businesses when they most need it.
Showcasing the very best examples of design
from around the world, this year's shortlist has
once again captured the spirit of the moment
and I am sure will continue to inspire and
have resonance for years to come.
I hope that you enjoy exploring the nominations
and choosing your personal favourites.

INTRODUCTION
Deyan Sudjic

When the Design Museum launched the Beazley
Designs of the Year project ten years ago,
the title was carefully considered to reflect that
it was the design that we were looking at,
rather than singling out an individual designer.
It was an acknowledgement that a design –
whether it is a website or a car, a piece of
furniture or a work of architecture – can seldom
be considered the work of one person. How
something is made and how it is used are an
essential part of the story.
The process for the awards starts with the vigilance
of international design practitioners, curators
and critics, who, throughout the year, are alert to
new developments in both their area of expertise
and their region of the world. Their nominations,
received by the Design Museum and reduced
to a shortlist of sixty to seventy projects, are then
presented in an exhibition at the museum, in
this accompanying catalogue and finally to an
independent jury who decide the year's winners.
In this catalogue are each of the shortlisted
projects in category order – architecture, digital,
fashion, graphics, product and transport –
accompanied by a rationale from its nominator
stating why, in their view, the project deserves
to be a Beazley Design of the Year.
As the director of the Design Museum, my advice to
the successive juries who have given generously
of their time in deciding on an appropriate
winner has been to think about how their choice
will look in a decade or more. Juries in the
past have included Antony Gormley and Antonio
Citterio, Ilse Crawford and Paola Antonelli,

all of whom have made impressive choices. Looking back over the years, Shepard Fairey – one of the few who really can be seen as an individual creator – and his Obama Hope poster, which is now part of the museum collection, sum up a very particular moment in the political history of the twenty-first century, and still pack a strong emotional punch. GOV.UK, the British government website, was a reminder of how much design is now about the immaterial. The One Laptop Per Child project, the very first Design of the Year, was in its time a worthy winner, but has turned out to be a concept quickly made obsolete by the dizzying speed of change.

And we have missed some obvious pieces: while the iPhone was at least nominated, it did not, as some might expect in hindsight, win the Design of the Year award. From the viewpoint of 2017, it's clear that it has done more than anything to change the way that we all live now.

Buckminster Fuller once suggested that if you wanted to predict the future, the best way is to design it yourself. What we think of as the future is already with us, and a lot of the newest developments that are shaping it are here in this remarkable collection of designs.

PAST DESIGNS OF THE YEAR WINNERS

DESIGNS OF THE YEAR AWARD 2016
Better Shelter
Johan Karlsson, Dennis Kanter, Christian Gustafsson,
     John van Leer and Tim de Haas in partnership
     with IKEA Foundation and UNHCR

DESIGNS OF THE YEAR AWARD 2015
Human Organs-on-Chips
Donald Ingber and Dan Dongeun Huh, Wyss Institute,
     Harvard, USA

DESIGNS OF THE YEAR AWARD 2014
Heydar Aliyev Cultural Centre
Zaha Hadid Architects, UK, for the Republic
     of Azerbaijan

DESIGNS OF THE YEAR AWARD 2013
GOV.UK website
Government Digital Service, UK

DESIGNS OF THE YEAR AWARD 2012
London 2012 Olympic Torch
Edward Barber and Jay Osgerby for the
     London Organising Committee of the Olympic
     and Paralympic Games, UK

DESIGNS OF THE YEAR AWARD 2011
Plumen 001
HULGER and Samuel Wilkinson, UK

DESIGNS OF THE YEAR AWARD 2010
Folding Plug
Min-Kyu Choi, UK

DESIGNS OF THE YEAR AWARD 2009
Barack Obama Poster
Shepard Fairey, USA

DESIGNS OF THE YEAR AWARD 2008
One Laptop Per Child
Yves Béhar of fuseproject, USA

DESIGN: A RISKY BUSINESS
Glenn Adamson

It was over three decades ago now that Ulrich Beck published his unlikely bestseller *Risk Society: Towards a New Modernity* (1986). The book has seemed more prescient with each passing year. Beck argued that modern societies are no longer primarily organised around direct profit and loss, or supply and demand. Rather, they are oriented to the management of uncertainty. As we become ever more aware of risks, from natural disasters to economic downturns, and ever better at calculating their likelihood, we work harder and harder to protect ourselves. Often, in a global economy, this means shifting risk elsewhere, on to other people in other places. This is the exertion of power in the future tense.

Beck's analysis can be applied to many disciplines, but its relevance to design is particularly profound. For design is one of the few means we have at our disposal actually to eliminate risk, rather than just hand it on to someone, somewhere else. Design can be defined as the improvement, or optimisation, of things. But this doesn't just mean making them safer, cheaper and better. It also means reshaping the systems in which design happens. Like a stone dropped in a pond, every new design sends ripples through the world, via the multiple currents of production, distribution, use and waste. By reshaping the stone, we change the pattern. In this way, through design, we can reduce environmental impact, improve access to information and promote cross-cultural communication, all through sheer ingenuity.

This theme of risk seems particularly appropriate to this particular edition of Beazley Designs of the Year, the tenth in the series, for two reasons. First, any milestone is a good occasion to take a step back, and assess. How predictive have these exhibitions been over the past decade? As Deyan Sudjic relates in the introduction to this catalogue, it has not been a faultless track record. Some influential designs went unrecognised. Some award-winners never fulfilled their initial promise. Like anything else, design looks very different in retrospect, in the rear-view mirror of settled history.

Yet the overall intention of the series, to evaluate design at its moment of inception, remains a vitally important task. Hindsight is of little use if we don't translate it into foresight. That is what this exhibition series is all about. It is a collective sticking out of the neck, one in which the nominators, the museum, the jury and of course the designers themselves must all hazard guesses about what might make the world a better place. We will often be wrong. But we might just be right, and so we keep on trying.

There is a second reason to emphasise risk: the past year itself. It's been a hell of a time. The refugee crisis, warfare both ideological and actual, election results that dismayed millions, spiking awareness of impending climate change: we are living through risk society in action. The headlines are reflected in the exhibition's content. There are, as one might have expected, numerous expressions of political dissent: posters, protest banners, pussyhats. (That all of these originate from the left side of the political spectrum may also be unsurprising: not many reactionaries go to design school.)

To judge from the selection, the plight of Syrian
and African refugees has been the single issue
of greatest concern to designers this year.
We include projects that trace the whole of the
migrant experience. Why do refugees flee their
homes? A digital recreation of Saydnaya,
a Syrian 'dark prison', provides crushing virtual
testimony. What can be done about the tragic
loss of life in the Mediterranean? Avy, a search-
and-rescue drone, is one proposed solution.
How to ease the transition of refugees into new
lands, where they may or may not be welcome?
There's an app for that – truly – but the exhibition
also includes traces of the now-destroyed
Calais Jungle, indicating the dystopian reality
of young migrants' experience.
Finally, how might the refugee crisis affect
European culture in the long run? One possibility
is suggested by the artist Emeka Ogboh, who
imagines Germany in thrall to a beer brand
called Sufferhead, tailored to African immigrants'
tastes (it's a stout brewed with chilli peppers).
Ogboh's mordant infomercial for Sufferhead
imagines it becoming so popular that all domestic
German beers begin to fall out of fashion.
The project challenges us to imagine refugees
as an exciting influx, not an existential threat.
Strange that this should seem the stuff of fiction.
The range of these responses, from pragmatic
problem-solving to sharp satire, is indicative.
Design has many ways to cope with risk. The
strategy depends on who is doing the designing.
Sometimes, particularly in activist contexts,
people who are not professional designers look
to apply their skills, driven by a sense of political
urgency. Ogboh is an example of this, as are
the originators of the Pussyhat Project,

screenwriter Krista Suh and architect Jayna Zweiman. So too is the photographer Wolfgang Tillmans, whose elegiac poster campaign failed to avert Brexit, but remains an indelible visual statement of its moment.

The exhibition traverses many forms of design agency, from individual pursuits like these all the way up to massive institutional commitments. Ulrich Beck rightly criticised governments and multinational companies for shifting risk off their books and on to an unsuspecting citizenry. But as the exhibition attests, many governmental and corporate initiatives do successfully apply the principle 'first, do no harm'. Honda's Moto Riding Assist prevents motorcycles from tipping over and trapping their riders. Piaggio's robotic carrier on wheels, Gita, should be a genuine boon to its users, particularly the elderly.

Driverless public transport, another prominent theme in this year's show, is another example of heavily capitalised design that has the real potential to benefit society, by reducing pollution and traffic deaths. Google, working with the graphic-design company Monotype, deserves recognition not only for its futuristic Project Jacquard, but also for the Noto typeface, free to use and compatible with any world language. As for governmental initiatives, it is encouraging to note that potentially life-changing products such as the Scewo stair-climbing wheelchair continue to receive public funding. And of course there's Graham, the unforgettable face of Australian road safety – proof that government agencies have a sense of humour, too ... if only occasionally.

Yet, as significant as small-scale and large-scale design agency may be, it is the middle ground that remains most promising. As has been true in previous editions of the exhibition, the vast majority of this year's nominated projects originated in independent design studios. Leaving aside highly topical, but not exactly transformative, selections (like Pokémon GO or Kanye West's latest fashion line), the pattern is even more pronounced. One might argue that this emphasis on atelier-based practice reflects the prejudices of our nominators, but I disagree: independent design firms have numerous competitive advantages that help them achieve genuinely transformative ideas. Free of the constraints that often inhibit corporate design departments, they can tailor specific projects to actual social need, rather than the imperatives of an existing product line.

If anything, the independent start-up is a more viable proposition than ever. Previously, designers had to combine a portfolio of early-adopter clients, angel investors and grants to see them through the research-and-development phase. That pattern still holds – BuffaloGrid, a remote power-charging station, was funded in that manner. Today, however, a good enough idea can often attract sufficient crowdfunding, or enough pre-orders, to go straight into production. Waverly Labs' Pilot translating kit, Refugee Text and Graviky Labs' AIR-INK have all been resourced in this way.

New production techniques, particularly 3D printing, also help to reduce up-front investment because they are inherently compatible with production on demand. Other designers, continuing a trend that has been gaining strength in recent years, take matters literally into their own hands. Studios like gt2P (Great Things To People) in Chile, and architects like Francis Kéré, who hails from Burkina Faso, draw on local materiality and expertise as building blocks of creativity. Eric van Hove, a flexibly minded artist and engineer, has undertaken a campaign of import substitution, training artisans in Morocco to make vehicles and even functioning motors as replacements for shoddy imports. For now his results are shown in museums and galleries, but if you live in Marrakech, they could soon be coming to a street near you. These are further pathways that designers are taking to manage risk: by starting with their own business models.

Thus far I have been discussing design in relation to ongoing and future risk. But it can be equally effective when things have already gone wrong. Perhaps the most powerful examples of this ameliorative role in the exhibition are two buildings: Erlend Blakstad Haffner's Utøya Hegnhuset and David Adjaye's National Museum of African American History and Culture (NMAAHC). At first glance, they would seem to have little in common, apart from their sheer beauty. One is a quiet, modestly scaled building on a wooded Norwegian island, the other a monumental ziggurat, clad in bronze-coated metal, set dramatically on the Mall in Washington, DC. Yet both are shaped around past trauma. Utøya was the site of a horrific massacre in 2011, a mass shooting in which sixty-nine people (many of them children and teenagers) were killed. The central storyline of the NMAAHC, meanwhile, is the long struggle to win freedom from slavery. Both buildings are intensely emotional experiences: built meditations on the nature of evil, and the vital importance of community. These are places to reflect on humanity at its worst and best.

Beyond such direct confrontations with the past,
architects deal with the even more basic fact of
entropy. This could be seen as the flip side
of risk, in that nothing is more certain.
All our works will fall into decay, eventually.
This Ozymandian truth seems to have been
especially resonant this year. When our present
seems out of joint, perhaps it feels that much
more important to hold on to where we have
been. Several projects here are oriented
to this goal, including the Five Dragons Temple
in China, by Urbanus, and OMA's Fondaco dei
Tedeschi in Venice. Croft Lodge Studio,
conceived by Kate Darby and David Connor,
is an eighteenth-century cottage that has fallen
into picturesque ruin; the architects encased it
in a protective shell, preserving its fragile beauty.
In designing her last masterpiece, the Antwerp
Port House, the visionary Zaha Hadid went to
even more extreme lengths to emphasise the
preservation of an existing structure.

At a certain point during the run of Beazley Designs
of the Year 2017, a jury will meet to determine
the awards. They will select recipients in
six overall product categories, as well as an
overall winner. (We will also have a public vote,
designating a 'people's choice'.) As the exhibition's
curator, I don't envy the jurors one bit. Every
nominated project has its own claim to
recognition, whether that is based in aesthetics,
ethics or simply relevance.

I do have one choice to make though, and that is how
to end this essay. For this purpose, I choose
the Refugee Nation Flag designed by Yara Said
– herself a Syrian migrant, now living in
Amsterdam. Blaze orange with a single black
band, it was inspired by life vests, worn by

so many refugees as they seek a new home.
Said wore one herself during her passage
to safety. At some point in the future, we will
look back at the events of 2016 and 2017, far
wiser about their ultimate meaning. But when
it comes to understanding the times, I don't
think we will ever do any better than this:
a thin fabric, whipped by the wind, standing
somehow for hope.

DESIGN BY THE NUMBERS:
A GRAPHIC OVERVIEW OF THIS YEAR'S NOMINEES
Eleanor Watson

Since its inception in 2008, Beazley Designs of the Year has stood as a barometer of contemporary design, allowing us to record and forecast changing trends across this complex, multi-disciplinary field. Now in its tenth year, it seems important for the exhibition to engage in a certain level of self-scrutiny. In this spirit, we have taken stock of this year's nominated projects in terms of the human, material and financial resources that made each of them possible. It also invites us to ask the fundamental question: how are designers working today?

The findings presented in the following set of infographics are in many ways unsettling. The limited geographical diversity, for example, while certainly reflective of our own unintended bias as a British institution, is a reminder of how far the design world still has to go in order to achieve a truly global outlook. While great designers are born the world over, nine out of the world's top ten design schools are currently based in the United States and the United Kingdom. Talent and innovation are therefore being pooled in extremely limited, affluent areas, rather than in places of greatest need. Equally sobering is the gender imbalance, with women making up only twenty-five per cent of the lead designers from this year's projects. Believe it or not, this is a higher level of representation than the UK national average.

More encouraging is the design world's approach to environmental issues, with a considerable number of practices using waste material to create new products, while others move towards low-impact, local and underused resources. This trend is overshadowed, however, by the sheer number of designers who are moving away from the material world altogether, with nearly twenty per cent of this year's projects existing only in digital form. From traffic light systems for self-driving cars to exhibitions presented through virtual reality, the design world is becoming ever more populated by the intangible.

The most striking conclusion to emerge from the data is perhaps one which we've already known – namely, that design is singularly equipped to deal with change. In an increasingly fast-paced and complex world, designers have continually demonstrated an ability to react rapidly and efficiently to changing circumstances, with sixty-five per cent of nominated designs being completed in less than two years. Design teams are also largely revealing themselves as nimble, small-scale enterprises, with over seventy-eight per cent of this year's designs being created by a team of less than ten people. Finally, a strong reliance on crowdfunding is setting a hopeful pitch for design in years to come, as new frameworks of production and consumption allow for more direct social and political engagement. The possibilities of design are all around us, and it's time for all to engage.

A REFUGE FOR YOUNG
MIGRANTS, NO MORE
A BEAUTIFUL RUIN KEPT
SAFE AND SOUND
A TANG DYNASTY
TEMPLE, RESURRECTED
A SENSITIVE RESTORATION
IN THE HEART OF VENICE
A BUILDING THAT HELPS
HEAL A COMMUNITY
A HIGH SCHOOL MADE
FROM THE GROUND UP
A MODULAR HOUSE
FOR AN ANCIENT CITY
A FINAL MASTERPIECE
FROM ZAHA HADID
A THEATRE RENOVATION
THAT TELLS ITS OWN STORY
A TRIBUTE TO THE AFRICAN-
AMERICAN EXPERIENCE
A WATER TOWER THAT
HARVESTS THE SKY
A CITY BUILT OF MEMORIES
A BRIDGE THAT CONNECTS,
ON EVERY LEVEL

THE CALAIS BUILDS PROJECT

DESIGNER Gráinne Hassett with migrants
living in the Calais Jungle and students of
Architecture from the University of Limerick
NOMINATOR Nathalie Weadick

The Calais Builds Project captured the needs,
culture and hopes of the residents of the Jungle
refugee camp. Architect Gráinne Hassett,
along with students from the University of
Limerick and local migrants, designed and built
a major community infrastructure, including
a Women and Children's Centre and the Baloo's
Youth Centre. The build crew were from Ireland,
Scotland, England, Sudan and Afghanistan.
The buildings were functional and provided
safety and dignity when it was most needed,
but were demolished by the French Government
and their inhabitants once again displaced.
Even though the structures are now gone,
they were prototypes for how to bring stability
to an extreme and inhumane, yet all too
common, global scenario. The story of the Calais
Builds Project asks pertinent questions about
the political, social and environmental concerns
of architecture, and of society in general.

A REFUGE FOR YOUNG MIGRANTS, NO MORE

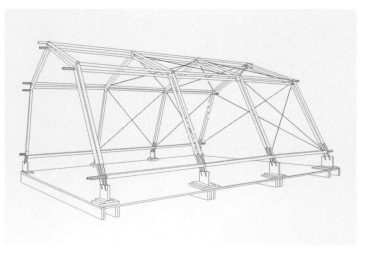

CROFT LODGE STUDIO

DESIGNER Kate Darby Architects and
    David Connor Design
NOMINATOR Kate Goodwin

A dilapidated 300-year-old cottage in Leominster,
Herefordshire, has been reappropriated to
surprising effect as a studio space with guest
accommodation. This imaginative project
encapsulates the remains of the eighteenth-
century building, leaving many of its original
features – including dead ivy, rotten timbers
and old birds' nests – intact. The ruin has
been wrapped in a new outer envelope of
black corrugated metal. In most places there
are two walls, two windows and two roofs, both
old and new. From the outside, it looks like a
simple rural shed, while inside, new white walls
contrast starkly with the roughness of the
existing building. Completed for just £160,000,
this modest project displays an intriguing
and skilful approach to conservation. Here the
old lives within the new, cobwebs and all.

A BEAUTIFUL RUIN KEPT SAFE AND SOUND

THE ENVIRONMENTAL ENHANCEMENT OF THE FIVE DRAGONS TEMPLE

DESIGNER Urbanus
NOMINATOR Aric Chen

Given China's spotty record with historic preservation,
architect Wang Hui's Five Dragons project
for a rural temple complex in Shanxi province
dating to the Tang dynasty (618–907 AD) offers
a ray of hope. For years, the long-derelict temple
and grounds were walled off and inaccessible,
a form of 'protection' that alienated local villagers
and only worsened the state of the buildings.
By designing a series of understated squares,
courtyards and walkways, as well as linking
the historic structures with each other and their
surroundings, Wang deftly created new public
spaces, restoring the temple compound to its
place at the centre of village life. Temple and
residents now sustain each other. What's more,
there is no theme-park atmosphere here.
Instead, the use of local materials, and well-
integrated installations about the history of the
temple and classical Chinese architecture,
lend just the right whiff of an outdoor museum.

A TANG DYNASTY TEMPLE, RESURRECTED

FONDACO DEI TEDESCHI

DESIGNER OMA
NOMINATOR Johanna Agerman Ross

Ever since their exhibition *Cronocaos* at the Venice
Architecture Biennale in 2010, OMA has had
an intellectual preoccupation with preservation.
The sixteenth-century Fondaco dei Tedeschi,
right by the Rialto Bridge on the Grand Canal
in Venice, is one of a handful of projects that
bring OMA's thinking into practice. Originally
a German trading post, it most recently served
as Venice's post office, before being bought
by the Benetton Group in 2008. Over a period
of eight years the square plan, centred around
a courtyard, has been carefully restored and
altered to create a department store like no
other – Venice's first such building. 'The ambition
was to have the starting point in everyday life,'
says OMA's Ippolito Pestellini Laparelli. 'To have
somewhere where you can buy a book, drink
a coffee, but also have luxury shops inside.'
As such it is a place for tourists and locals alike.
Visitors can engage with the layers of Venice's
history within the fabric of the building
itself: from the medieval wall in the courtyard,
the eighteenth-century brickwork and the 1930s
concrete supports to OMA's twenty-first-
century interventions.

A SENSITIVE RESTORATION IN THE HEART OF VENICE

HEGNHUSET, MEMORIAL AND LEARNING CENTRE ON UTØYA, NORWAY

DESIGNER Blakstad Haffner Arkitekter
NOMINATOR Tim Abrahams

The island of Utøya still looks like a paradise, lying low and wooded in the Tyrifjorden. Yet here Anders Breivik murdered sixty-nine young Labour activists. At the heart of this youth camp, which is continuing as a haven for thought and solidarity, sits a remarkable building, designed by Blakstad Haffner Arkitekter, that has answered the apparently impossible question: how do you inhabit a place where something so bad has happened, while still bearing testimony to the victims? The Hegnhuset is a very architectural way of dealing with this profound dilemma. A double colonnade surrounds the brutally severed form of the Kafébygget, a site where a large number of activists were killed. The colonnade creates a building line with a new library and canteen, while the old café has had its front facade removed up to a depth of several feet, the maimed bulk wrapped within the new structure. The building brings the past into line with a new plan, retaining the most significant parts of the old structure in a sculptural representation of violence.

A BUILDING THAT HELPS HEAL A COMMUNITY

LYCÉE SCHORGE SECONDARY SCHOOL

DESIGNER Kéré Architecture
NOMINATOR Papa Omotayo

On rare occasions, a building represents something bigger than the beauty of its form and the articulation of its function. As a Nigerian architect, I find it interesting to see how 'African architecture' is understood and portrayed: it is important to have examples that challenge Western narratives. To me, the new African architecture seems to lie in bridging the generational tension that exists between two conceptions of the local, one old and one new. The Lycée Schorge Secondary School exemplifies this unique combination. The school reimagines tradition and reconsiders what we consider modernity, through form, function, materiality and participation. It offers a new language for an architectural identity and expression that feels familiar, while at the same time presenting imaginative solutions that are relevant for the future. In this way, the Lycée becomes a vehicle through which wider African concerns – socio-economic, cultural and environmental – are addressed. Kéré's work is an essential part of the dialogue on global architecture, as it offers a new aesthetic for local aspirations, a new sense of what local-global 'African architecture' can be.

A HIGH SCHOOL MADE FROM THE GROUND UP

MRS FAN'S PLUG-IN HOUSE

DESIGNED BY People's Architecture Office
NOMINATED BY Beatrice Leanza

Mrs Fan's Plug-In House, one of an ongoing series, is a prefabricated urban solution originally developed by the Beijing-based People's Architecture Office as an alternative regenerative approach for the city's historic hutong districts. It tackles issues of architectural preservation and infrastructural upgrading without disrupting the socio-cultural ecosystem of resident communities. The Plug-In House, developed in 2016, is an independent habitation unit that can be fully customised and assembled on site; it originated in a pilot effort in 2013 with the support of the Dashilar Project, a government initiative consisting of a renovation method for traditional courtyard houses, aimed at avoiding blanket demolition. The proprietary prefabricated panels of the Plug-In House incorporate insulation and interior and exterior finish into one moulded part that can be locked to the next part with a single hex. The final structure integrates septic tanks to handle sewage. The project addresses the housing crisis with cost-effective and energy-efficient technologies, whose affordability prevents the undesired relocation of low-income populations.

A MODULAR HOUSE FOR AN ANCIENT CITY

PORT HOUSE

DESIGNER Zaha Hadid and Patrik Schumacher
of Zaha Hadid Architects for Antwerp
Port Authority
NOMINATOR Jonathan Glancey

The early twentieth-century Antwerp Docks fire
station was originally to have been crowned
with a tall tower visible over what are now
twelve kilometres of docks. Today it is adorned
with a striking, self-supporting, ship-like
superstructure, faced with 2,000 diamond-
shaped windows – some clear, some opaque,
and many faceted. It provides elegant (and
highly energy-efficient) office accommodation
for port staff who, previously, had been scattered
around this historic diamond-trading city, which
today handles a quarter of Europe's container
shipping. Below Zaha Hadid's glistening decks,
the brick fire station has been intelligently
renovated, serving as a reception lobby and
further offices. The interplay between the two
structures is dramatic yet sure footed, reflecting
the inherent dynamism of the Belgian port of
which it is now architectural hub and anchor.

A FINAL MASTERPIECE FROM ZAHA HADID

SALA BECKETT THEATRE AND
INTERNATIONAL DRAMA CENTRE

DESIGNER Flores & Prats Architects
NOMINATOR Kate Goodwin

A project five years in the making, this scheme by
Catalan architects Ricardo Flores and Eva Prats
transformed Barcelona's old Peace and Justice
Cooperative Building into a new home for the
Sala Beckett Theatre. The building, which dates
back to the 1920s, has been brought back to life
through a series of interventions that preserve
its original spatial characteristics while adding
new floors to serve the needs of a modern
theatre company. The theatre is given a street
presence with a large corner opening and a large
foyer connects the building's three levels of
classrooms, exhibition halls, offices, rehearsal
rooms and performance spaces. Details
of the building's previous use emerge as layers
are peeled away – from brightly coloured
tiling to ornate plasterwork. The sympathetic
interventions and playful colour palette sit
comfortably against bare plaster walls, exposed
timber and original rose windows. It is a playful
and courageous project, delighting and
surprising in equal measure.

A THEATRE RENOVATION THAT TELLS ITS OWN STORY

SMITHSONIAN NATIONAL MUSEUM OF AFRICAN AMERICAN HISTORY AND CULTURE IN WASHINGTON, DC

DESIGNER Adjaye Associates, The Freelon Group, Davis Brody Bond, SmithGroupJJR for the Smithsonian Institution
NOMINATOR Abraham Thomas

Occupying one of the last undeveloped sites on the National Mall, this museum opened after decades of efforts to commemorate African American history that date back to a campaign over 100 years ago led by black veterans of the Civil War. The design takes its cues from both African and American histories of craftsmanship. The multi-tiered corona form of the building evokes traditional Yoruban caryatid columns, while the ornamental exterior panels draw from historical lattice ironwork found in the American South, often created by enslaved Africans. The angles echo the nearby Washington Monument, underscoring the African origin of its obelisk form, and offering a provocative visual counterpoint to the neo-classical facades of surrounding federal buildings. The museum's location becomes even more poignant with the knowledge that it is situated on the site of a former slave market. Carefully positioned apertures create framed views of both the Lincoln Memorial and the Washington Monument, reminding visitors that the origin story of America is inseparable from the African American experience.

A TRIBUTE TO THE AFRICAN-AMERICAN EXPERIENCE

WARKA WATER

DESIGNER Arturo Vittori
NOMINATOR Jane Withers

No matter how arid the climate, moisture always
exists in the air; the question is how to harvest
it. Warka Water cleverly combines a rain butt,
fog catcher and dew collector in the form of
a twelve-metre-tall bamboo tower that supports
a sleeve of water-gathering mesh able to amass
100 litres of clean drinking water every day.
Italian designer Arturo Vittori developed the
project in a remote village in northeastern
Ethiopia, mimicking nature's water-collecting
techniques, as seen in beetle's shells, the leaves
of lotus flowers and spider's webs. This eighty-
kilogram, open-source design can be constructed
without scaffolding or machinery at a cost of
$1,000 (less than £800). Once trained, villagers
are easily able to build as many towers as
needed. The name of the project comes from the
Warka tree, an expansive fig endemic to
northern Ethiopia: the tower's canopy emulates
its shady branches, under which communities
traditionally gather.

A WATER TOWER THAT HARVESTS THE SKY

WELTSTADT – REFUGEES' MEMORIES AND FUTURES AS MODELS

DESIGNER Schlesische27 International Youth, Arts and Culture Center in collaboration with Raumlaborberlin and the SRH Hochschule der Populären Künste (hdpk)
NOMINATOR Jana Scholze

This exhibition was the result of a year-long project, in which 150 young refugees worked with eight Berlin workshops to create models of buildings at a 1:10 scale. They show the buildings that these people left behind and remember: homes, schools, factories, houses of prayer, restaurants. Through the use of recycled materials, they are made to appear rather realistic. This process of memory-making was not just one of reconstruction, however. Next to ruins unmistakably demolished by war are houses, some partly furnished, that serve as reminders of good times and dreams of the future. The models are shaped by the experiences of war, escape, refuge and displacement, and reflect those 'broken histories'. Making models – a typical part of any design process – is here used as a tool for individual reflection and vision. The exhibition, which could be interpreted as a single potential 'world city', provides an opportunity for communication and exchange. It allows visitors to imagine the deep trauma and fear, but equally the hopes and dreams, of their new neighbours.

A CITY BUILT OF MEMORIES

WIND AND RAIN BRIDGE

DESIGNER Donn Holohan with students from the
University of Hong Kong and Peitian Community
Craftsmen
NOMINATOR Nathalie Weadick

Wind and Rain Bridge, designed by Donn Holohan
and co-created by local people, is a combination
of indigenous construction techniques and
thoughtful design that resulted in a powerful
piece of rural place-making. Holohan, together
with students from the University of Hong Kong,
worked with a community in an isolated region
of southern China, who became dislocated
after a major flood in 2014. Completed in 2016,
the scheme is successful in bringing together
the skills of these local people – long traditions
of native wooden building – with contemporary
engineering methodologies. Collectively they
have created a space that is beautifully
crafted and designed, while contributing to
the future of the settlement and the well-being
of its inhabitants.

A BRIDGE THAT CONNECTS, ON EVERY LEVEL

A TYPEFACE FOR EVERY
LANGUAGE ON EARTH

A HUMAN DESIGNED TO
SURVIVE A CAR CRASH

A COMPANY AT THE
FRONTIER OF 3D PRINTING

AN OUT-OF-BODY ENCOUNTER
WITH ART DECO

A VIDEO GAME THAT
RESCRIPTS PUBLIC SPACE

A NEW LOOK FOR
ENGLISH FOOTBALL

A REVOLUTIONARY TECHNOLOGY
FOR MANUFACTURE

A CORRECTIVE TO
SEXIST TEXTS

AN INFORMATION
HOTLINE FOR REFUGEES

A VIRTUAL TOUR OF A
BRUTAL SECRET PRISON

GOOGLE NOTO

DESIGNER Google and Monotype
NOMINATOR Catherine Flood

Google Noto is a family of open-source typefaces
encompassing 800 languages and over
100 different writing systems. Type designers,
linguists and language communities all over
the world have collaborated to create a
body of typefaces that retain a cohesive feel
while capturing the vitality and history of
individual scripts. In a few cases this is the first
time that a rare or 'dead' language has been
given a digital typeface and thereby the
possibility of being preserved online. The name
Noto is shorthand for 'no more tofu' – tofu being
the little boxes that appear when your device
doesn't support a particular font. Tofu can cause
a significant breakdown in communication,
particularly for those using less-common
languages. The Noto typefaces expand the
possibility for people all over the world to create
and share digital information in the language
of their choice. By allowing multilingual content
to be integrated harmoniously on screen,
they invite communication across barriers of
language and culture.

A TYPEFACE FOR EVERY LANGUAGE ON EARTH

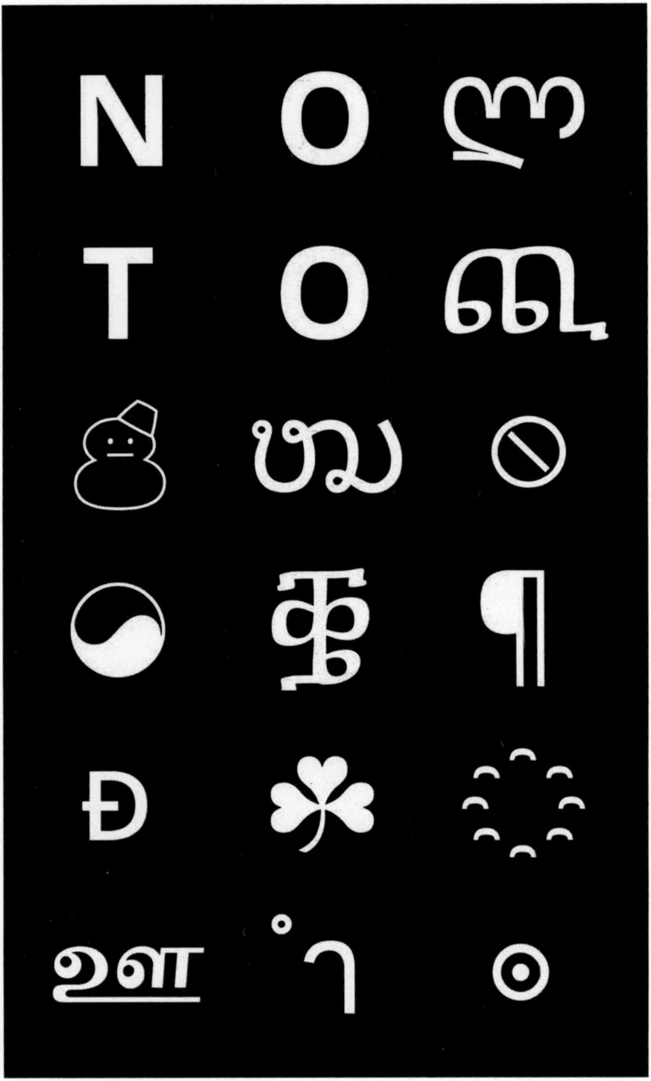

MEET GRAHAM: THE ONLY PERSON DESIGNED TO SURVIVE ON OUR ROADS

DESIGNER Patricia Piccinini in collaboration with Dr Christian Kenfield, Dr David Logan and Clemenger BBDO for Transport Accident Commission (Victoria, Australia)
NOMINATOR Mandi Keighran

Meet Graham is an Australian road-safety campaign, by Clemenger BBDO Melbourne for the Australian Transport Accident Commission. It shows how human bodies would have to evolve to survive the impact of a traffic accident. The artist Patricia Piccinini was commissioned, along with a leading trauma surgeon and a road-crash investigation expert, to create a surreal, life-like sculpture called Graham, to be displayed around the country and online. The display included an augmented-reality experience, using Google Tango devices, offering a richer way to discover what is beneath Graham's skin and to explore the decisions behind his anatomy. I have nominated the campaign for the way in which it successfully combines elements – including interactive artwork, website and educational tools – to create an unforgettable public-service announcement and a reminder of just how fragile our bodies are.

A HUMAN DESIGNED TO SURVIVE A CAR CRASH

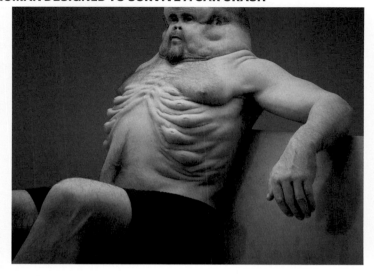

OTHR

DESIGNER Joe Doucet, Dean Di Simone
and Evan Clabots
NOMINATOR Steven Learner

Think of OTHR as a decentralised Bauhaus for
the twenty-first century. The New York-based
firm is not only transforming our notion of
3D printing by producing premium made-to-
order domestic objects in porcelain, bronze and
steel, but is also rethinking the entire design and
production process. Recognising that today's
studio is not necessarily a physical space, OTHR
works with leading designers around the globe,
using Dropbox and Skype to replace in-person
design meetings. With the cost of living in major
creative capitals skyrocketing, this working
method may soon become a reality for designers
everywhere. In addition, all of OTHR's objects
are produced on demand and sold only online,
greatly reducing the environmental impact
associated with producing and holding inventory.
More than just creating useful and beautiful
products, OTHR has cleared a path to the current
evolution of our creative culture, embracing
technologies, techniques and modes of
communication that extend design practice.

A COMPANY AT THE FRONTIER OF 3D PRINTING

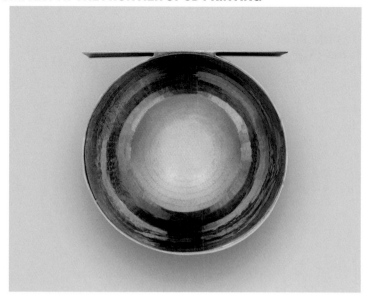

PIERRE CHAREAU: MODERN ARCHITECTURE AND DESIGN

DESIGNER Diller Scofidio + Renfro
NOMINATED BY Felix Burrichter

The collaborative efforts between the curator Esther da Costa Meyer and the architects Diller Scofidio + Renfro resulted not only in a beautiful and thoughtful exhibition on Chareau's design legacy, it also served as a stunning example of how technology can be used in a subtle and beautiful way to bring to life for a contemporary audience work of historic importance. As a designer, Chareau was quietly radical. While some of his contemporaries attempted to prescribe their grand schemes to entire cities, Chareau preferred to test and apply his ideas on a very intimate, domestic scale. The designers for the exhibition in New York used this idea of intimacy to create a series of spatial vignettes enhanced by virtual reality. Pieces of furniture taken from one of Chareau's most famous works, the Maison de Verre in Paris, were arranged in clusters and, with the help of VR goggles, visitors to the exhibition were transported into the different spaces of the house. The exhibition provides visitors with a direct experience that no model or drawing could provide.

AN OUT-OF-BODY ENCOUNTER WITH ART DECO

POKÉMON GO

DESIGNER Niantic
NOMINATOR Abraham Thomas

Bursting on the scene during the 1990s with its memorable slogan 'Gotta Catch'Em All' and its fantastical universe of 'pocket monsters', Pokémon has become the highest-grossing media franchise of all time, beating Star Wars, Harry Potter and James Bond. Exploiting nostalgia for the brand's early days, Pokémon GO was developed for mobile devices as a location-based augmented-reality game, utilising GPS capabilities to allow players to capture, train and battle virtual creatures which appear on screen as if in the same real-world location as the player. With its addictive world of 'Poké Balls', lure modules and potions, the game became a global phenomenon during the summer of 2016. With many 'Poké Stops' and 'Pokémon Gyms' located at sites of historical and cultural interest, the game encourages players to rediscover their neighbourhoods and communities, creating a curiously contemporary form of urban exploration. Inevitably, the game garnered its fair share of controversies – with stories of distracted players being robbed at gunpoint or requiring emergency rescue from caves – and even led to some cities passing legislation to regulate its use.

A VIDEO GAME THAT RESCRIPTS PUBLIC SPACE

PREMIER LEAGUE ON-AIR BRANDING

DESIGNER DixonBaxi
NOMINATOR Abraham Thomas

The Premier League is a brand that reaches over a billion fans worldwide. In early 2016, they dropped title sponsorship and developed a fresh visual identity with a vivid palette of clashing colours and patterns, and a simplified version of the iconic lion logo. DixonBaxi brought these elements to life on air, creating a 'de-corporatised' look and feel that challenged the conventions of sports graphics. It resulted in dynamic show titles and a custom motion-graphics system inspired by the fluid movements of play on the field. Designed to work across both broadcast and digital platforms, the branding has a distinctive information-design aesthetic inspired by video-game interaction graphics and motion overlays, which feels reflective of a broader cultural intersection between professional sports and video gaming. Professional gaming has become an important extension of mainstream sport brands, leveraging huge opportunities within the exploding eSports market. Manchester City, West Ham and Paris Saint-Germain all employ professional FIFA gamers, building competitive franchises that can tap into a global sports phenomenon projected to produce revenues of $1.5 billion (£1.2 billion) and audiences totalling 300 million by 2020.

#CHELEI

Chelsea

Leicester City

Sunday 15 May

"AND I'LL TELL YOU HONESTLY. I WILL LOVE IT
IF WE BEAT THEM. LOVE IT!"
KEVIN KEEGAN

RAPID LIQUID PRINTING

DESIGNER Self-Assembly Lab at
Massachusetts Institute of Technology (MIT),
Christophe Guberan and Steelcase
NOMINATOR Libby Sellers

Such is the speed at which we travel through
technology: even before it has had the chance
to fulfil its potential to democratise design,
3D printing has already been surpassed.
Its production scale (small), speed (slow) and
materials (built layer by layer) have all been
bested by the next generation of prototyping:
Rapid Liquid Printing. Created by MIT's Self-
Assembly Lab in collaboration with American
furniture company Steelcase, Rapid Liquid
Printing involves a robotic apparatus depositing
extruded lines, suspended in a tank of gel.
The material holds its own form and chemically
cures as it is injected – the object is literally
drawn into existence. Early experiments,
such as the furniture designs by Christophe
Guberan launched during the 2017 Milan
Furniture Fair, explored printing in a variety
of materials, including plastics, rubbers and
polyurethanes. Rapid Liquid Printing can
produce unprecedentedly large-scale objects
in a fraction of the time previously required;
the only constraints are the size of the tank
and stockpiles of gel.

A REVOLUTIONARY TECHNOLOGY FOR MANUFACTURE

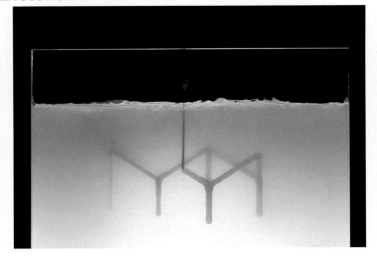

PROFESSIONAL WOMEN EMOJI

DESIGNER Agustin Fonts, Rachel Been,
Mark Davis, Nicole Bleuel and Chang Yang
NOMINATOR Alex Bec

Like them or not, it is impossible to ignore the role emoji now have in our day-to-day communication, with ninety per cent of the world's online population using them. With the demand for our little pictogram friends being so high, the need for a suitable representation of genders, races and interests shifts from being an important design consideration to one of complete necessity. This year, it was wonderful to see Google, one of the companies most able to ensure that these tools are an accurate representation of the millions of people around the world who use them, step up and make a difference. Previously, male emoji included a detective, a police officer and a doctor, while the options for female emoji included a princess, a bride and a girl getting a haircut – not exactly the most empowering or accurate depiction of females in the workplace. One small step for gender equality in the workplace, but a big leap for emoji everywhere.

A CORRECTIVE TO SEXIST TEXTS

REFUGEE TEXT

DESIGNER Kåre MS Solvåg, Caroline Arvidsson
and Ciarán Duffy
NOMINATOR Simona Maschi

Refugee Text is a chatbot for refugees. It takes
verified and trustworthy information from
organisations such as the United Nations High
Commissioner for Refugees (UNHCR) and
makes it available on demand to any refugee
with a phone. The team spent the latter part
of 2015 and early 2016 researching the systems
in place in Europe for refugees. Surprisingly,
one of the largest unaddressed needs among
refugees and humanitarian organisations
alike was for simple information: even when
there is an official policy, it can be difficult
for refugees to understand what it means for
them. Similarly, volunteers are often unsure
of recent changes in laws affecting refugees.
RefugeeText addresses these issues with
a simple turn-key chatbot that is personalised
to each person's own particular situation.
Editing and translating is managed through
a custom Chatbot Management System, which
allows organisations to operate chatbots
across multiple languages, online and via SMS.
The system has been in use by UNHCR Northern
Europe since October 2016 and has already
delivered information on asylum requirements
to thousands of refugees across Europe.

AN INFORMATION HOTLINE FOR REFUGEES

SAYDNAYA: INSIDE A SYRIAN TORTURE PRISON

DESIGNER Forensic Architecture and
      Amnesty International
NOMINATOR Karen Verschooren

Forensic Architecture is one of the most intriguing
contemporary research agencies. It bridges
the fields of design, politics and jurisdiction.
Borrowing methodologies from the realms
of architecture, design, film, activism and theory,
their research produces spatial analysis that has
provided evidence for international prosecution
teams, political organisations, NGOs and the
United Nations. For Saydnaya: Inside a Syrian
Torture Prison, Forensic Architecture researchers
worked together with survivors to reconstruct
the physical structure of a prison near Damascus,
and their experiences within it, using architectural
and acoustic modelling. The prison model
and related audiovisual material offer an
intimate and chilling confrontation with the
reality of Syrian detention facilities. Run by
the government, these places are unmonitored
black holes: tens of thousands of people have
been tortured and thousands have died.
The project is part of a wider campaign led by
Amnesty International, calling on the Syrian
government to allow independent monitors
into its detention centres and urging other key
players to weigh in on the debate.

A VIRTUAL TOUR OF A BRUTAL SECRET PRISON

FASHION

A COAT WOVEN
FROM OCEAN WASTE

A HIGH-TECH INTERACTIVE
TEXTILE FOR ANY GARMENT

A HIP-HOP STAR'S
FASHION FORAY

A CATWALK MODEL
UNLIKE ANY OTHER

A HIGH-PERFORMANCE
HIJAB

A HANDMADE SYMBOL OF
WOMEN'S SOLIDARITY

ECOALF

DESIGNER Javier Goyeneche, Founder and
President of ECOALF and Carolina Blazquez,
Head of Innovation and Sustainability
NOMINATOR Sam Baron

Ecoalf is an upcycling project based in Spain,
a country whose extensive coastline is exposed
to sea pollution. Involving local fishermen
but reaching out to consumers worldwide,
this project highlights the full design process,
from initial idea to final products that are
respectful, intelligent and inventive. Ecoalf
removes waste from the sea and transforms
it into new materials (pellet, yarn, fabric).
From these, the Madrid-based studio creates
a selection of wearable goods: from footwear
to clothes via accessories, all with a very
contemporary design and look that works
with our day-to-day activities. Turning debris
into premium-quality raw materials is a way
of conveying to the fashion industry and its
consumers – all of us – a deep message: it calls
on us to care about our world and be conscious
of the consequences of our actions, all of
which can be analysed and shifted to fit in
a uniquely positive ideology that uses design
and technology to navigate a route from
recycling to retail.

A COAT WOVEN FROM OCEAN WASTE

LEVI'S COMMUTER TRUCKER JACKET WITH JACQUARD BY GOOGLE

DESIGNER Google with Levi's
NOMINATOR Pamela Golbin

Project Jacquard, conceived and created by Google, makes it possible to incorporate interactivity into any textile using standard industrial looms. Any garment or other object can be lined with this connective fabric, transforming it into a surface that is sensitive to touch and gesture. Jacquard yarns, which combine thin metallic alloys with natural and synthetic materials such as cotton, silk or polyester, are visually indistinguishable from normal contemporary yarns. They can be woven on any industrial loom, allowing designers to use them as they would any other fibres, adding new layers of functionality to their designs. Bespoke interactive areas can be woven at precise locations anywhere on the fabric. Miniaturised circuits capture touch data that is wirelessly transmitted to any device, allowing simple hand gestures to trigger actions on your smartphone. The Commuter Trucker Jacket, created in partnership with Levi's, is the first interactive denim jacket.

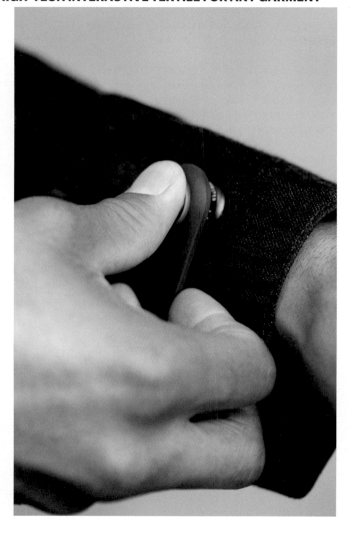

LIFE OF PABLO POP-UP STORES

DESIGNER Kanye West and Mat Vlasic for Bravado
NOMINATOR Ben Terrett

Coinciding with his album *The Life of Pablo* and
Saint Pablo tour, West launched a pop-up
project across twenty-one international cities to
sell Pablo-branded merchandise. The locations
of the stores were revealed on Twitter by West
twenty-four hours before they opened, and
included London, Amsterdam, Berlin, Singapore,
Cape Town, Melbourne, New York and Toronto.
This extravaganza resulted in customers lining
up for hours to get their hands on T-shirts
and hoodies with the brand's recognisable
Gothic font, designed by Cali Thornhill DeWitt.
The design is inspired by memorial sweatshirts
made in Mexican-American communities for
deceased loved ones, with further inspiration
from LA. West is constantly changing the rules
of music promotion: musicians have long made
more money from merchandise than selling
music, but Kanye explicitly inverted this by
holding a big 1990s-style launch event for the
merchandise, and quietly launching the
actual album for free on streaming services.

A HIP HOP STAR'S FASHION FORAY

'THE RITE OF SPRING / SUMMER / AUTUMN / WINTER' NEW OBJECT RESEARCH

DESIGNER Aitor Throup
NOMINATOR Diane Pernet

Aitor Throup is fascinated with what he calls 'New Object Research' rather than with fashion per se. The Argentinian-born designer is known for his collaborations with the band Kasabian, including artwork for their album *For Crying Out Loud*, for which he sampled and deconstructed his own record collection. Throup continued exploring new ground in his catwalk show 'The Rite of Spring/Summer/Autumn/Winter', a collaboration with puppet designer James Perowne. Together they created life-sized marionettes to model the clothing, a novel way to explore the articulation of the human body through dress. The performance was divided into three acts, like a theatrical production, with additional drama provided by the setting: the Holy Trinity Church in London. At the entrance was an installation of cast bodies, wearing more of Throup's garments, piled up and spray-painted in white. 'Through defacing my own work,' Throup said, 'I am disregarding its current surface value whilst allowing it to peacefully rest.'

A CATWALK MODEL UNLIKE ANY OTHER

NIKE PRO HIJAB

DESIGNER Rachel Henry, Baron Brandt,
     Megan Saalfeld and Brogan Terrell for Nike
NOMINATOR Wayne Hemingway

Nike Pro Hijab was designed with the aim of
     providing a performance garment for Muslim
     women. Working alongside athletes such
     as figure skater Zahra Lari, Nike has developed
     a lightweight hijab made of a single layer
     of polyester mesh. The material is soft and
     stretchy, and the design includes tiny opaque
     holes for optimal breathability, as well as an
     elongated back to ensure it stays in position.
     The hijab is adjustable, and comes in two sizes
     and various colours. This design serves to
     provide culturally appropriate and comfortable
     attire for professional Muslim athletes, as
     well as eliminating one of the barriers that stops
     Muslim girls participating in sports. Simple,
     stylish, functional – how come it has taken
     so long for a product like this to hit the market?
     The apparently simple piece of cloth gives
     women the confidence to try something new.

A HIGH-PERFORMANCE HIJAB

PUSSYHAT PROJECT

DESIGNER Krista Suh, Jayna Zweiman, Kat Coyle
and Aurora Lady
NOMINATOR Libby Sellers

The simplicity of the Pussyhat Project belies its audaciousness. From the outrage that followed President Donald Trump's toxic and aggressively sexist admission of 'grabbing 'em by the pussy' came the most visually effective and internationally recognised symbol of protest this century – the pink pussyhat. The vision of co-founders Krista Suh and Jayna Zweiman, the project was launched ahead of the Women's March on Washington in January 2017, as hundreds of thousands of people were encouraged to download a rudimentary, open-source pattern to knit a pink hat. Drawing on the broad history of knitting as a tool for non-violent political activism (or 'craftivism', a term coined by Betsy Greer in the early 2000s), Suh and Zweiman believed that the process of making, sharing and wearing a hat would be a demonstration of solidarity for women's rights and political resistance. By harnessing the power of social media, the project spread like pink wildfire; never before had craftivism been witnessed on this scale. The sea of pink marching on cities around the world that day was more than just a moment – it became a movement.

A HANDMADE SYMBOL OF WOMEN'S SOLIDARITY

A GRAPHIC DEPICTION OF
WORKPLACE INEQUALITY

A SPECIAL, AND URGENT,
MAGAZINE ISSUE

AN ELECTION POSTER
FOR THE SOCIAL MEDIA AGE

A WAY TO SAY WE'RE
STILL TOGETHER

A MUSIC LABEL THAT'S
REINVENTING THE INDUSTRY

A POLITICAL CAMPAIGN
WITH A POETIC TOUCH

A PUBLIC SERVICE FOR
PROTESTORS

AN ARCHITECTURE JOURNAL
WITH A PLAYFUL FORMAT

A FLAG FOR
THE STATELESS

A NEW PUBLISHING PLATFORM
FOR GRAPHIC DESIGN

A LOGO THAT GOES
THREE WAYS

A NEW IDENTITY FOR
WALES

FINDING HER

DESIGNER IC4DESIGN with DDB Dubai
for UN Women Egypt
NOMINATOR Anniina Koivu

Finding Her is a campaign that mimics the maddeningly labyrinthine scenes of *Where's Wally?* Rather than searching for the red-and-white striped Wally, Finding Her asks readers to seek out a lone woman among crowds of male workers. The project highlights the startling gender disparity in Egypt's three biggest up-and-coming industries: science, technology and politics. The three ads, created by the DDB Dubai agency and Japanese IC4DESIGN for United Nations Women in Egypt, appeared in Egyptian magazines at the end of 2016. They are a creative way to show just how seriously underrepresented women are in the country's labour market: only twenty-three per cent of Egypt's workforce, among the lowest percentage rates in the world, according to UN Women. The message on each illustration reads: 'It shouldn't be this hard to find women in the workplace.' Let's hope these puzzles prove less timeless than *Where's Wally?*

A GRAPHIC DEPICTION OF WORKPLACE INEQUALITY

'FRACTURED LANDS', THE NEW YORK TIMES MAGAZINE, 14 AUGUST 2016

DESIGNER Jake Silverstein, Editor-in-Chief,
Gail Bichler, Design Director, and Matt Willey,
Art Director, for *The New York Times Magazine*
NOMINATOR Simon Esterson

One way for printed magazines to survive is to break
out of their mould, think smarter and experiment
more. Under editor Jake Silverstein and design
director Gail Bichler, the weekly *New York Times
Magazine* has been publishing a series of special
issues where it steps away from its regular
design and tries something different with both
form and content. Recent examples have
included a feature on high-rise buildings with
distinctive vertical graphics, and a whole issue
in comic-book form. The 'Fractured Lands' issue
of August 2016, designed by art director Matt
Willey, is dramatically austere and book-like,
with monochrome typography and bold
chapter openers. It is an appropriate design for
a single 40,000-word piece of journalism about
the recent history of the Arab world by Scott
Anderson. The pages are punctuated by
twenty black-and-white images by Magnum
photographer Paolo Pellegrin. The issue ran
without any advertising interrupting the feature.

A SPECIAL, AND URGENT, MAGAZINE ISSUE

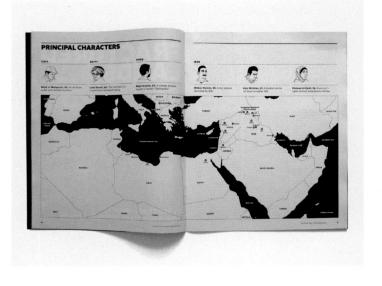

IBIZA MYKONOS JEREMY CORBYN (POLITICAL POSTERS)

DESIGNER Michael Oswell
NOMINATOR Ben Terrett

Remember in the 1980s, when the big advertising agencies used to make iconic posters at election time? The only decent posters this year were by Michael Oswell, a designer not officially affiliated to any particular party and definitely not to an advertising agency. He uses the tropes of modernism to poke fun at the huge gap between political rhetoric and how people typically speak on the internet. Out of this comes a pace and an optimism, which feel similar to the groundswell that has allowed web-based groups like Momentum to gain traction. Oswell gives you all the ephemeral nature of the internet and modern politicians – in a poster. The posters, out of necessity, exist as preprint screenshots. They are rapidly assembled according to a loose template, are assigned a title, a format, a speculative print process, and are then sent out into the wild of the internet where they are left to sink or swim.

ME & EU

DESIGNER Nathan Smith and Sam T Smith
NOMINATOR Micha Weidmann

ME & EU is a collection of postcards written
and designed by British creatives that
are to be sent across Europe, with the aim
of remaining connected after the Brexit
referendum. The project was initiated and
published by Nathan Smith and Sam T Smith
of GBH London. It is a great reflection of how
political engagement can be extended through
design. The electoral events and the spread
of fake news throughout the past year have
provoked various guerrilla designs by people
who want to express their own points of view,
or simply want to expose the truth as they
see it. ME & EU encourages people to become
part of this movement, with a design that
shows great aesthetic variation and makes
some clever graphic statements.

A WAY TO SAY WE'RE STILL TOGETHER

THIS POS
CARD HAS
NO
BORDERS

A PERSONAL MESSAGE FROM ME TO EU.
TO KEEP IN TOUCH SEND TO:
58 CHURCH LANE, LONDON, SW17 9PR
FOR MORE INFORMATION VISIT: WWW.MEANDE

N.A.A.F.I

DESIGNER Alberto Bustamante a.k.a. Mexican Jihad
NOMINATOR José Esparza

The genre-bending underground record label
N.A.A.F.I goes far beyond music. Through its
seven years of existence, N.A.A.F.I's radical and
political approach has dramatically changed
the nightlife landscape of Mexico. In its early
days, the label's eclectic sound was understood
as a confrontational stance against the drug-
related insecurity throughout the country.
Now it sounds like the soundtrack of a growing
non-conformist, anti-heteronormative generation,
which has slowly infiltrated mainstream
culture through the bold use of design as a
communication tool. Often appropriating official
government and corporate identities, N.A.A.F.I
announces its events through social media, and
produces high-quality merchandise that is both
irreverent and provocative. Though now a
recognisable brand, the label expresses both
political discomfort and a sort of careless
attitude towards institutions of power. Through
its comprehensive idea of design, N.A.A.F.I
expands the understanding of the graphic field
in a way that truly captures the spirit of a new
and progressive creative community.

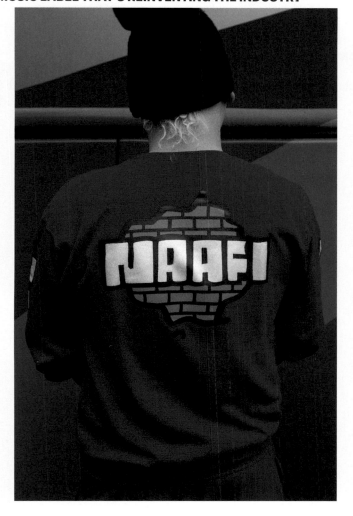

PRO-EU ANTI-BREXIT POSTER CAMPAIGN (VOTE REMAIN 23 JUNE), 2016

DESIGNER Wolfgang Tillmans, Between Bridges
NOMINATOR Catharine Rossi

In June 2016, Britain took part in a vote that would decide the future of the nation: the European Union Referendum. Standing out in the noise created by both sides of the campaign was Vote Remain, Wolfgang Tillmans' impassioned pro-European Union initiative. The German photographer produced a collection of posters, as well as T-shirts and an explanatory letter. Available to download for free from his website, the striking posters combined emotive statements with abstract landscape imagery that urged people to reject today's escalating extremism in favour of the Union's values. Tillmans' designs were partly a reflection of his disappointment with the official Remain campaign, which proved well founded, as British voters narrowly decided to leave. This project is significant as a failure – a lesson in how design needs to communicate more effectively – and, more positively, exemplifies design's increasing politicisation, which breeds hope for much-needed change.

PROTEST BANNER LENDING LIBRARY

DESIGNER Aram Han Sifuentes in collaboration
with Verónica Casado Hernández, Ishita Dharap
and Tabitha Anne Kunkes
NOMINATOR Catherine Flood

This library provides workshops for people to make
protest banners and is a resource for those
who want to borrow and use them. The project
enables protest against Trump's political
agenda in a number of meaningful ways.
First, by providing a communal space where
people can see, talk and sense solidarity.
Second, the concept of a library holding banners
that will be used and re-used recognises there
are no quick fixes to the political struggles
we face today. In an era of easy 'clicktivism',
the very durability of a textile banner signals
a commitment to sustained resistance and
movement-building. Third, the project
acknowledges that the democratic right to
protest is unequal. For undocumented people,
for example, the consequences of arrest can
be too high to take part. In this context, making
a banner that someone else will carry on to
the streets offers a means of speaking out and
a role in stitching the fabric of social change.

A PUBLIC SERVICE FOR PROTESTORS

REAL REVIEW

DESIGNER Jack Self, Editor-in-Chief, and
OK-RM (Oliver Knight and Rory McGrath),
Creative Directors
NOMINATOR Alex Milton

Real Review is a quarterly magazine that explores
'what it means to live today'. Funded via
Kickstarter, the project has built an engaged
readership who have responded enthusiastically
to the premise of an accessible platform for
robust debate around contemporary architecture.
Real Review's distinctive, vertically folded format
physically refers to an unfolded and expanded
practice of architecture. It responds to the
functional distribution requirements of the post,
while celebrating the tactile joy of print in a
digital age. The magazine rejects the prevailing
notion of architecture and design magazines as
lifestyle-focused artefacts designed for the
coffee table; instead, it offers a content-driven,
newspaper-inspired, four-column platform that
playfully treats the page like real estate.
Actively addressing the political, economic,
social and cultural role of architecture today,
this publication's creative process is an exercise
in extracting maximum value and meaning
within tight constraints and planning parameters,
very much reflective of a life lived today.

AN ARCHITECTURE JOURNAL WITH A PLAYFUL FORMAT

THE REFUGEE NATION FLAG

DESIGNER Yara Said with The Refugee Nation
    for Amnesty International
NOMINATOR David Kester

How would I cope, were I forced to flee my
    home country for fear of my life? Yara Said
    is an artist who graduated in 2014 from the
    University of Damascus. What should have been
    a time of creative and personal development
    for her was instead defined by civil war.
    Fleeing Syria in one of the many boats carrying
    refugees, she wore the orange-and-black
    lifejacket that is a signature artefact of this
    modern-day exodus. Having settled in
    Amsterdam, Yara was approached by a newly
    formed organisation, The Refugee Nation,
    to create a flag to represent refugee athletes
    at the 2016 Rio Olympics. Yara's simple and
    striking design became an act of hope, and an
    emblem for refugee athletes who marched
    to a new anthem, watched by millions
    globally. This design story is also about one
    woman's experience transcending her situation
    and creating an enduring symbol in the face
    of an intolerable global crisis.

A FLAG FOR THE STATELESS

UNIT EDITIONS

DESIGNER Tony Brook, Adrian Shaughnessy
and Patricia Finegan
NOMINATOR Quentin Newark

Tony Brook, his wife Patricia Finegan and his
friend Adrian Shaughnessy all love books,
but were frustrated working with contemporary
publishers, finding them 'controlling and risk
averse' and not disposed to treating design
seriously. So the trio founded Unit Editions
to make new books as well as they can possibly
be made. Their mantra is: design books that
no one else would think to publish. They operate
out of the studio of Spin – Brook and Finegan's
design group – and use the internet to create
their buying audience. Whether it be Kickstarter
projects, social media launches or sales on their
website, this independence from the standard
publishing model also gives them freedom from
the conventional approach to content. The trio
goes where their curiosity takes them, responding
to design that moves, intrigues and amazes
them – and then conveying such sentiments to
new readers.

A NEW PUBLISHING PLATFORM FOR GRAPHIC DESIGN

VISUAL IDENTITY FOR REYKJAVIK ART MUSEUM

DESIGNER karlssonwilker inc.
NOMINATOR Sarah Archer

Consistency is the logo's primary job: it cuts through
visual noise, and across barriers of culture and
language. By this logic, the new mark of the
Listasafn Reykjavíkur (Reykjavik Art Museum)
might not be a logo in the traditional sense at all:
its most striking characteristic is that it never
looks the same. Yet this happens to be a sensible
way to represent the institution, since it exists
in several places at once. The Listasafn has three
locations: the main complex, a modern art
museum in a city park, and an artist's former
home. With increased touristic interest
in Iceland in recent years, the Listasafn's
leadership discovered confusion on the part
of visitors, who didn't realise that the three sites
comprised a single museum. The solution from
karlssonwilker was to create a rotating triangular
logo, with the sides identifying the three
locations. The logo conveys the idea that the full
Listasafn experience can only be had as each
site comes into view.

A LOGO THAT GOES THREE WAYS

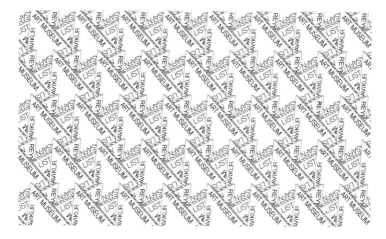

WALES NATION BRAND

DESIGNER Smörgåsbord
NOMINATOR Will Hudson

Dylan Griffith and his team at Smörgåsbord have given Wales a comprehensive rebrand to be proud of. Addressing every brand touchpoint, including core marque, bespoke typeface, tone of voice, photography guidelines and experiential initiatives, they have created a compelling and visually consistent approach to help reveal new and engaging stories, complementing the rich history, beauty and culture of Wales in the process. The re-visioned Wales nation brand was developed in response to the Welsh Government's ambitions to develop a refreshed and integrated strategy for promoting Wales to the world as a place to visit, trade, invest and live. What began essentially as a tourism campaign has swelled into a nation-wide revamp, providing the whole country with a unifying visual identity with the contemporary and reductive rendering of the familiar Dragon icon at its core.

A NEW IDENTITY FOR WALES

AN INK SUCKED OUT
OF CAR EXHAUST PIPES
                    AN ILLUMINATED
                    MODULAR ALPHABET
A RESCUE DRONE
FOR REFUGEES AT SEA
                    A WAY TO POWER UP,
                    ANYTIME, ANYWHERE
AN URBAN DANCEFLOOR
FOR ALL TO ENJOY
                    A SUPER-BIODEGRADABLE
                    CHAIR
A SIMPLE STICKY TAPE
THAT MAKES ANYTHING FUN
                    A WAY TO TALK FACE
                    TO FACE IN ANY LANGUAGE
A SEAT MADE OF
CHILEAN LAVA
                    A CRIB THAT
                    ROCKS ON CUE
A SET OF BENCHES,
FASHIONED FROM CLOTH
                    A FAKE PRODUCT THAT
                    GETS AT A DEEPER TRUTH
AN END (AT LAST) TO
FIDDLING WITH SCREWS

AIR-INK

DESIGNER Graviky Labs
NOMINATOR Nicolas Roope

Issues around climate change and pollution are fraught with political complexity. The consequence is indifference. What we can't see can't hurt us – that is, until it does. Making the invisible visible is what design often does, and AIR-INK couldn't be a more literal example. It begins with a filter mounted on the exhaust pipe of a vehicle or diesel generator. This device captures up to ninety-five per cent of the tiny invisible particles in the pollutant, which would otherwise blacken our streets and our lungs. This material is refined and then used as a pigment for ink that can itself be used to communicate. While not a conventional design as such, AIR-INK is a potent gesture that connects people to the urgent issue of climate change, bringing poetic inspiration to a daunting global challenge.

AN INK SUCKED OUT OF CAR EXHAUST PIPES

ALPHABET OF LIGHT

DESIGNER BIG (Bjarke Ingels Group) for Artemide
NOMINATOR Bernard McCoy

BIG's Alphabet lamp is an innovative lighting system
consisting of two basic elements – a combination
of straight and curved lines of light – which
add up to a new seamless typeface. It can be
used to write any sentence, number or graphic
signage. Both an expressive tool and a functional
light source, Alphabet can also be seen as a
light sculpture, complementing any architectural
space. The design is liberating, in the sense
that you no longer have to hire someone
to shape signs for you. It is a smart system of
inter-changeable pieces, where the simplicity
of form belies technological complexity. Each
strip comprises of a thin central aluminium core
which supports two LED strips emitting light on
opposite sides. These modular elements are
fused together with concealed electromagnetic
joints, creating a seamless effect without
shadows or discontinuities.

AVY SEARCH AND RESCUE DRONE

DESIGNER Paul Vastert, David Wielemaker,
Christian McCabe and Patrique Zaman
NOMINATOR Ingeborg de Roode written
in collaboration with Jeanette Bisschops

Those who fled their homelands in recent years
had to make a dangerous journey across
the Mediterranean. The often decrepit,
overcrowded boats they used did not always
make it to the other side: last year alone,
3,500 refugees perished attempting the sea
crossing. The Avy Search and Rescue Drone was
specifically designed to help these waterborne
refugees. The drone is capable of flying long
distances and detecting vessels, and can drop
life jackets, lifebuoys, food supplies and
medication. This design gives drones, which
are often associated with warfare, a much
more positive role. It can really help people.
According to the designer, once in full production,
Avy could also be used to search for poachers,
and therefore it could do some good for animals
as well. It is indeed an innovative design –
and also a beautiful one.

A RESCUE DRONE FOR REFUGEES AT SEA

BUFFALOGRID

DESIGNER Daniel Becerra
NOMINATOR Matt Webb

While mobile phones may improve economic and
social prospects, in parts of rural India power
is unreliable. BuffaloGrid distributes electricity,
one phone charge at a time. At its core
is a luggable battery, kept topped up either
by agents who travel village to village, or using
solar panels. Customers purchase power by
sending a premium-rate text message
and – using Internet of Things technology – a
USB charging port is unlocked for one full
charge. Previously, phone owners living off-grid
would have had to waste time and money
travelling to more expensive electricity
sources. The agents get a cut of each purchase,
incentivising them to travel further off-grid.
BuffaloGrid makes a profit, too, building up funds
for more batteries. This is not a charity. The
shape, weight and handle of the battery allow
it to be easily carried by agents on bicycles; the
payment system avoids the need for cash.
The BuffaloGrid battery is not just a successful
design when it comes to manufacturing and
aesthetics: it represents a complex network of
incentives and behaviours, economics and
people, reflected in lithium-ion and red plastic.

A WAY TO POWER UP, ANYTIME, ANYWHERE

DANSBANA! VÅRBY GÅRD

DESIGNER Dansbana! (Anna Fridolin, Anna Pang
and Teres Selberg) for Huddinge kommuni
NOMINATOR Kieran Long

Dansbana! is a small urban space in Vårby,
a southern suburb of Stockholm, designed
by three Stockholm-based architects: Anna
Fridolin, Anna Pang and Teres Selberg.
It is a terrazzo dancefloor, carefully detailed
with a high-quality sound system made of
bright and beautiful metal-clad speakers.
Anyone can connect their phone via Bluetooth
to the system and dance. The three architects
were inspired to form the Dansbana!
organisation after research showed that new
public spaces built for young people in Sweden
were overwhelmingly sports fields, and therefore
dominated by boys. Dansbana!, developed
through dialogue with local dance groups, is
intended to be a place for young girls. The name
refers to a well-known Swedish historical type:
the public dancefloors in the 'people's parks'
that were the hearts of their communities
in the early twentieth century. Dansbana!, with
its ebullient exclamation mark, is the work
of designers ready to rethink for the twenty-
first century the legacy in terms of public
space of Swedish welfare-state architecture.
The designers are now working on a second
Dansbana! in Södertälje.

AN URBAN DANCEFLOOR FOR ALL TO ENJOY

FLAX CHAIR

DESIGNER Christien Meindertsma for
LABEL/BREED
NOMINATOR Mateo Kries

Christien Meindertsma's Flax Chair shows that
it is still possible to make a surprising and
radically innovative piece of furniture. The chair
is constructed from boards composed of flax
and a sustainable glue. After being cut out of
this board material, the pieces are bent into their
form. The result is a chair that convinced me at
first sight: it looks wonderfully lightweight and
elegant, yet is pared down to the extreme
minimum. This look is derived from the chair's
innovative material. Meindertsma's Flax Chair
is an extraordinary example of a new material
for furniture that leads to new methods of
construction and manufacturing. It reminds
me of design icons like Willy Guhl's 1954 garden
chair for Eternit, made of fibre-reinforced
cement, or Alberto Meda's Light Light Chair
from 1987, made of carbon fibre. The Flax
Chair is Dutch design at its best: a minimalist
approach combined with experimental curiosity
and great sensitivity to new materials.

A SUPER-BIODEGRADABLE CHAIR

NIMUNO LOOPS

DESIGNER Anine Kirsten, Max Basler and
Jaco Kruger
NOMINATED BY Micha Weidmann

Nimuno Loops tape has been developed to allow
Lego builders to place their creations on
the walls, the ceiling, the furniture – pretty
much anywhere. It can be cut to any
desired length, and it bends sideways as
well. While not developed (or even officially
sanctioned) by the Lego company, it allows for
an even more creative engagement with
their plastic bricks and other components,
already loved for their abundance of
possibilities. This is a great example of how
the functionality of an existing product can
be extended through responsive design.

A SIMPLE STICKY TAPE THAT MAKES ANYTHING FUN

THE PILOT TRANSLATING EARPIECE

DESIGNER Waverly Labs
NOMINATOR Philip Michael Wolfson

Asked to nominate for this year's awards, I had to consider what aspects of 'design' might lead to a higher quality of life on a worldwide level, not just a pretty object likely to serve no greater purpose than to stroke an ego or aid in the 'keeping up with the Joneses' mentality. That left me looking into the realm of new technology, where I was excited to find a number of compelling proposals on the verge of becoming real-world products. One of the most intriguingly advantageous designs is the Pilot speech translator earpiece. It is a bit of futuristic wearable technology right out of Star Wars or an Isaac Asimov story, which allows users to speak to each other in foreign languages and have the conversation translated directly and immediately into their ear. Pilot is being developed by Waverly Labs, an innovative products company created in 2014. They are incorporating the latest technologies in speech recognition, machine translation and wearable tech to allow users to converse without language barriers. Brilliant!

A WAY TO TALK FACE TO FACE IN ANY LANGUAGE

REMOLTEN

DESIGNER gt2P (Great Things To People)
    with Friedman Benda
NOMINATOR Frederico Duarte

In 2013, when the members of gt2P began
    experimenting with lava collected from the
    Chaitén and Villarrica volcanoes, they failed
    to find any relevant scientific and technical
    information to help them work with this highly
    abundant, native Chilean material. So they
    designed their own research process and
    manufacturing method. With funding from
    the Chilean state and support from New York
    City-based design gallery Friedman Benda,
    gt2P have since experimented with a series
    of material and typological objects that include
    porcelain lamps with melted lava switches,
    stoneware stools covered with ground lava,
    and solid lava tiles. For now, their findings
    have only materialised in high-end furniture.
    However, by 2018, the designers will release
    all the data collected during their research.
    They place greater value on knowledge than
    on commodities, and hope their work will spark
    future applications of lava in existing and new
    industries – in Chile and beyond.

A SEAT MADE OF CHILEAN LAVA

SNOO SMART SLEEPER

DESIGNER Yves Béhar of fuseproject
for Dr Harvey Karp's Happiest Baby
NOMINATOR Wayne Hemingway

In the first year of a child's life, it is estimated that parents lose an average of 1,000 hours of sleep. Ninety per cent describe themselves as tired or exhausted, and fifty per cent sleep only four to six hours a night. This sleep deprivation can lead to serious health issues for parents and babies alike. Fuseproject are tackling the issue with the SNOO Smart Sleeper. Based on the methods of world-famous paediatrician Dr Harvey Karp, the Sleeper is a mechanised bassinet that gently rocks babies back to sleep at the push of a button. Now that I am a granddad, I am reminded how important sleep is to a baby and to the parents (not to mention the grandparents). The SNOO crib combines technology, wit and mid-century-inspired classic design. What's not to love?

A CRIB THAT ROCKS ON CUE

SOLID TEXTILE BOARD BENCHES

DESIGNER Max Lamb for Really
NOMINATOR Emilia Terragni

The amount of waste that we accumulate daily is shocking. Much of what we buy is now cheap enough to be seen essentially as disposable, with products often easier to replace than to repair. I see it as our responsibility to recycle more and give greater consideration to things that would otherwise end up in landfill. We also need to be creative in the ways in which we recycle. Max Lamb gives an example of how. In collaboration with sustainability start-up Really and textile company Kvadrat, Lamb has created a new bench collection built from recycled textiles. The benches are produced using Solid Textile Board: a high-density material made from 'end-of-life' fabrics, mostly cotton and wool. Lamb has frequently used overlooked materials to create innovative designs, and here once again demonstrates the enormous potential of a waste product. These benches have an understated beauty that fully expresses the materiality of the boards. And while the technology used to transform the textiles into boards is not new, nor particularly complex, the opportunities for development and potential impact on the industry are incredibly exciting.

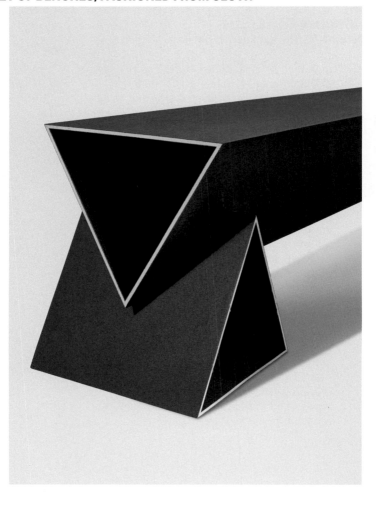

SUFFERHEAD ORIGINAL STOUT

DESIGNER Emeka Ogboh
NOMINATOR Ugochukwu-Smooth C Nzewi

Sufferhead Original, launched at the Kassel edition
of Documenta 14, is a smart combination
of micro-brewing, product design and artistic
social practice. It has a strong presence: a matt
black 33cl bottle in the imperial stout style
and a chic black-on-black label that feels at once
medieval, with its Gothic script in the German
Fraktur typeface, and contemporary. The beer
tastes of roasted malt, cocoa, coffee and honey,
with an unusual highlight flavour: a West African
pepper that gives it a fruity taste, heat and
originality. The product takes its name from
a 1981 track by the prescient Afrobeat musician
Fela Kuti, who bemoaned the harsh political
and economic conditions in Nigeria – a precursor
to mass emigration out of the country and
elsewhere in Africa. It is the experience of
Africans living in Europe, and the artist's own
position as an immigrant in Germany, that
inspired the project. By taking on a European
cultural and industrial tradition – making
beer – Ogboh inverts a similar strategy
of appropriation by Parisian avant-gardes
who turned to African masks and sculptures
to revitalise modern art.

WEDGE DOWEL

DESIGNER Knut Hagberg and
Marianne Hagberg, Inventors, Göran Sjöstedt
and Anders Eriksson, IKEA
NOMINATOR Ben Terrett

This is a really simple design that does away
with the need for screws, bolts, screwdrivers
and Allen keys when assembling IKEA furniture.
Developed in-house in IKEA's prototyping lab
and tested on a few products, it is now being
rolled out on every piece of furniture. It makes
products much easier to put together than
screws and bolts, and at the same time makes
them more stable. While users want furniture
that is quicker to put together, they also want
to be able to take it apart and reassemble it
easily – if they move house, for example.
This innovation makes that possible. And it
means manufacturing far fewer parts. The
wedge dowel is incredibly simple, user-centred
and even beautiful.

A TRAIN THAT RUNS
WITHOUT TRACKS

A ROBOTIC CARRIER THAT
FOLLOWS YOU LIKE A DOG

A MOTORCYCLE THAT
WON'T TIP OVER

A TRAFFIC SYSTEM FOR
THE SELF-DRIVING AGE

AN UPCYCLED SCOOTER
THAT DRIVES LOCAL INDUSTRY

A BUS WITHOUT
A DRIVER

A WHEELCHAIR THAT CLIMBS
UP AND DOWN STAIRS

A FUTURISTIC FLYING
WATER TAXI

AUTONOMOUS-RAIL RAPID TRANSIT (ART)

DESIGNER CRRC
NOMINATOR Aric Chen

The usual caveats apply: we don't know how well
this will really work, and the devil still lurks
in the details. But the Autonomous-Rail Rapid
Transit system, which earlier this year underwent
a much-publicised test-run in Zhuzhou, China,
is a self-driving electric vehicle that's guided
not by tracks, but a double-dashed line painted
on the street. Its seductiveness lies in its
promise of providing all the benefits of light rail
without the costs and other drawbacks of the
rails themselves. Instead, it runs on sensors
and rubber wheels, making it something of a
cross between a train, a bus and an urban
Roomba (those little robotic vacuum cleaners).
Though its technology seems straightforward,
its advantages have yet to be proven. But while
we all wait for flying cars and the Hyperloop,
it's good to know that people are still thinking of
incremental ways to improve mass transit, and
make it more affordable and accessible,
especially to smaller and less wealthy cities.

A TRAIN THAT RUNS WITHOUT TRACKS

GITA

DESIGNER Piaggio Fast Forward, led by Greg Lynn
NOMINATOR Nicolas Roope

We have been snacking on Hollywood's diet of robot-based fiction for decades, but these emotionally corrupted visions throw us way off the scent of where these technologies are actually headed. The common picture is one multipurpose, humanoid hassle-saver. The reality will be a plethora of more specific robotic products with dedicated roles and functions. Since the control technology is getting so cheap, why depend on a few multifunctional robots when any number of appliances could take on autonomous tasks? Here's one: Piaggio's Gita. Imagine having one of these at the airport, following you politely as you swan around fancy free. The Gita team didn't get carried away with the usual futurist vernacular, and instead created something that already feels quite approachable. This is critical to provide balance against the freakishness of these robotic stalkers, which will inevitably cause jaws to drop as they start to appear.

A ROBOTIC CARRIER THAT FOLLOWS YOU LIKE A DOG

HONDA MOTO RIDING ASSIST

DESIGNER Honda
NOMINATOR Max Fraser

Using self-balancing technology, engineers at Honda's Silicon Valley research-and-development department have created a new robotic motorbike that won't fall over and can even move without a rider. The aim is to greatly reduce accidents, particularly at low speeds, as well as improve the riding experience. The technology, named Moto Riding Assist, is programmed to disengage the handlebars from the front forks at speeds of three miles per hour or less. The control of the front wheel is then handled by the computer, which senses the bike leaning and makes tiny adjustments to counteract any tipping. It also adjusts the angles of the front forks, lowering the bike's centre of gravity to improve stability. Perhaps not necessary for experienced riders, Honda's prototype nevertheless takes away the anxiety of falling over. It is most beneficial to older users or those a little shorter in stature.

A MOTORCYCLE THAT WON'T TIP OVER

LIGHT TRAFFIC

DESIGNER Carlo Ratti at Senseable City Lab at
    Massachussetts Institute of Technology (MIT)
NOMINATOR Max Fraser

The pre-programmed traffic light system that we
    have always known could someday disappear
    – an eventuality made more likely with the
    introduction of this smart intersection system,
    developed by researchers at Massachusetts
    Institute of Technology (MIT) Senseable City
    Lab. As the reality of self-driving vehicles
    draws nearer, other elements of our road-based
    infrastructure require a wholesale reinvention.
    The researchers have developed slot-based
    intersections that could replace traditional traffic
    lights and significantly reduce queues and
    delays. The idea is based on a scenario in which
    sensor-equipped vehicles are allocated a
    crossing slot when approaching an intersection,
    with their speed adjusted before they pass
    through the intersection. At all times the
    vehicles' relative proximity is communicated,
    so that they remain at a safe distance from
    each other. The system is entirely flexible and
    adjusts with changes in the flow of traffic and
    pedestrians. The great breakthrough is in
    the efficiency of traffic flow, which is doubled
    with respect to current state-of-the-art traffic
    lights. Queues at intersections will become
    a thing of the past and pollution emitted from
    waiting vehicles will be greatly reduced.

A TRAFFIC SYSTEM FOR THE SELF-DRIVING AGE

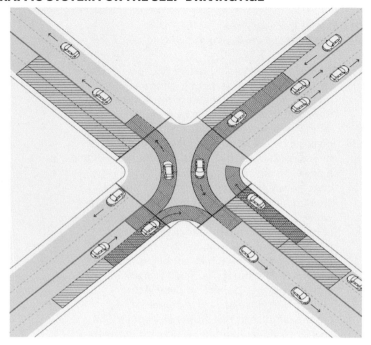

MAHJOUBA INITIATIVE

DESIGNER Eric van Hove
NOMINATOR Ugochukwu-Smooth C Nzewi

Eric van Hove's Mahjouba Initiative is a social and
entrepreneurial undertaking, centred on making
art. The project is intended to revolutionise
transportation in Morocco by creating an
indigenous motorbike industry. The project was
inspired by the Moroccan government's policy
on renewable energy (based on solar power) and
a desire to constructively engage the country's
craft-based workforce. In 2015, van Hove
created a first prototype motorbike, Mahjouba 1,
which borrows its basic design concept from the
ubiquitous and cheap Moroccan mopeds.
It is ninety per cent handcrafted from locally
sourced materials such as copper, camel bone,
cedar wood, resin, tin, recycled metals and
goat skin, and is powered by an electric
engine. Van Hove has since created three
other examples of this sturdy motorbike. The
ingenious project embraces the local network
of artisanal practice in Morocco, reimagining it
as a self-sustaining cooperative. The project
plugs these craftsmen into the formal industrial
economy, offering them a path to financial
stability and ultimately making a meaningful
impact on the local economy.

AN UPCYCLED SCOOTER THAT DRIVES LOCAL INDUSTRY

OLLI

DESIGNER Local Motors
NOMINATOR Philipp Rode

Olli is a self-driving microbus developed by the pioneering vehicle producer Local Motors, in partnership with public transport companies and using IBM technologies. It is innovative for two main reasons. First, it embraces autonomous vehicle technology to offer flexible urban mobility to the public, instead of retrofitting conventional automobiles. The electric vehicle, designed for up to twelve passengers, provides last-mile connectivity as part of a multimodal urban transport system. In this way, Olli can contribute to solving urban transport problems such as congestion, air pollution and excessive space consumption. Second, the vehicle is produced with 3D-printing technology, which radically reduces the time required to design, manufacture, test, mass produce and deliver vehicles, while also supporting decentralised, local fabrication. It allows for design flexibility too, with easy adjustments to the specific needs of customers or operational contexts. Olli has already been introduced in several American cities and is currently undergoing trials with the German railway company Deutsche Bahn in Hamburg and Berlin.

A BUS WITHOUT A DRIVER

SCEWO

DESIGNER Thomas Gemperle, Adrien Weber,
Naomi Stieger, Stella Mühlhaus,
Bernhard Winter and Pascal Buholzer at the
Swiss Federal Institute of Technology
NOMINATOR Wayne Hemingway

Scewo is a stair-climbing mobility device developed
by a group of students at the Swiss Federal
Institute of Technology. Using a retractable set
of rubber tracks, the wheelchair can safely
and smoothly travel both up and down stairs.
An extra pair of wheels at the rear allows users
to raise the chair so that they can engage with
others at eye level. The Paralympics, BBC idents
and the industrial design community have
started to treat disabled people as a community
that is part of life's rich tapestry. It is heart-
warming to see this brilliant wheelchair giving
users a hitherto unreachable level of
independence. The fact that the project was
self-funded by a group of university students
makes it even more remarkable.

A WHEELCHAIR THAT CLIMBS UP AND DOWN STAIRS

SEABUBBLES

DESIGNER Alain Thébault and Anders Bringdal
NOMINATOR Muriel Brunet

Seabubbles is a network of emission-free, noiseless and electric-powered water taxis that can be rented by the public using a transportation-sharing app like Uber. Employing the same physics as the Hydroptère sailing boat, the vehicle can 'fly' over choppy water to prevent seasickness. It is built with lightweight fibreglass and high-density foam, and has four foils attached to the hull to reduce any drag. When the boat reaches twelve kilometres per hour (7.5 miles per hour), it will hover above the surface of the water to avoid contact with waves for a smoother ride. The boat can seat up to five people, and a full-scale prototype was developed in 2016 by Alain Thébault and Anders Bringdal, a sailor and windsurfer respectively. The founders aim to have over a dozen vessels in service on waterways in Paris by 2017 and, starting in 2018, around the globe.

A FUTURISTIC FLYING WATER TAXI

ABOUT THE EXHIBITION DESIGN
Carmody Groarke and Micha Weidmann Studio

Carmody Groarke has designed the exhibition environment for Beazley Designs of the Year. It takes the shape of a sequence of sculptural cave-like forms, made from a sprayed paper pulp called Soundcel. This assertive materiality of the gallery was a response to the exhibition design brief, which specified a powerful spatial experience that would act as a strong counterpoint to the diversity of the nominated designs.

The existing gallery is completely abstracted into a series of amorphous spaces, blending continuously into one another. Rather than using conventional exhibition walls and plinths, the angled and curved spaces are covered entirely in Soundcel, which is usually spray-cannoned on to walls to provide insulation, smothering over the sculpted ledges and recesses that display the work. Its textured surface provides a beautiful, monolithic and cast-like quality to the exhibition spaces.

Micha Weidmann Studio has designed the orientation and signage for the exhibition, which are printed on to precision-cut, brightly coloured acrylic pieces. The signs slice into the papered surfaces, contrasting with the rough background of the exhibition environment.

The typography also follows the idea of the slicing movement with a tabulation system organising all content of the exhibition and the catalogue. The catalogue cover paper is made of recycled banknotes, reflecting the sensibility of a new material such as Soundcel, and also serving as a subtle reference to some of the themes in the exhibition.

NOMINATOR BIOGRAPHIES

TIM ABRAHAMS Writer about architecture and
design for *The Economist*. He is a contributing
editor at *Icon* magazine. He is also editor and
publisher at Machine Books.

JOHANNA AGERMAN ROSS Curator of
Twentieth Century and Contemporary Furniture
and Product Design at the Victoria and Albert
Museum. Before joining the museum she
founded and edited the quarterly design journal
Disegno and was an editor of the monthly
architecture and design magazine *Icon*.

SARAH ARCHER Contributing editor for the
American Craft Council's new journal,
American Craft Inquiry, a regular contributor to
Hyperallergic, and columnist for the *Magazine
Antiques* online. Her first book 'Midcentury
Christmas', which explores the material culture
of Christmas during the Cold War in the United
States, was published in 2016.

SAM BARON French creative director and designer,
embracing physical and digital projects with
a global approach. His innovative use of classic
techniques focuses on the relation between our
daily life and the existence of new archetypes.
His clients include Hennessy, Airbnb, La Redoute
and Vista Alegre. He has been the creative
director of Fabrica's design area since 2007.

ALEX BEC Managing director and co-owner of the HudsonBec Group, whose purpose is to enable creativity to thrive. The independent group includes media company It's Nice That, creative agency Anyways and educational resource Lecture in Progress.

MURIEL BRUNET Senior Director of Digital Projects, Economic Development and Innovation at the French Ministry of Education. She is an expert with over twenty years of experience in leading the development of digital projects. Over the past six years she has dedicated herself to fostering innovation and positive economic impact in the educational technology sector.

FELIX BURRICHTER German-born, New York-based creative director, curator, writer and editor. Originally trained as an architect in Paris and New York, in 2006 Felix founded the magazine *PIN–UP*. He also curates exhibitions, consults on design and architecture projects for various design brands, and contributes to numerous publications.

ARIC CHEN Lead Curator for Design and Architecture at M+, the new museum for visual culture under construction in Hong Kong's West Kowloon Cultural District.

FREDERICO DUARTE Portuguese design writer, critic and curator. He is currently conducting a doctoral research project on contemporary Brazilian design at the Victoria and Albert Museum and Birkbeck College in London. The exhibition he curated for MUDE, *How to Pronounce Design in Portuguese: Brazil Today*, is on display in Lisbon until December 2017.

JOSÉ ESPARZA Pamela Alper Associate Curator at the Museum of Contemporary Art Chicago. Previously, he was Associate Curator at the Museo Jumex in Mexico City. In 2013 he was co-curator of the Lisbon Architecture Triennial. Between 2007 and 2012 he held several positions at Storefront for Art and Architecture in New York and *Domus* magazine.

SIMON ESTERSON Editorial designer and art director of *Eye*, an international review of graphic design and *Pulp*, a magazine about people and paper for Fedrigoni.

CATHERINE FLOOD Prints curator in the Word and Image Department of the Victoria and Albert Museum, specialising in design and politics, and in 2014 she co-curated the exhibition *Disobedient Objects*. She has published on topics ranging from posters to nineteenth-century female illustrators.

MAX FRASER Design commentator across a wide range of media including books, magazines, exhibitions, video and events to broaden the conversation around contemporary design. As a consultant, he delivers content and strategy for a variety of public and private bodies in the United Kingdom and abroad.

JONATHAN GLANCEY Journalist, author and broadcaster. He was Architecture and Design correspondent for the *Guardian* from 1997 to 2012 and Architecture and Design Editor of the *Independent* from 1989 to 1997. His career began with the *Architectural Review* and he was a founding editor of *Blueprint* magazine.

PAMELA GOLBIN Chief curator of Fashion and Textiles at the Musée des Arts Décoratifs in Paris.

KATE GOODWIN Head of Architecture and Drue Heinz Curator at the Royal Academy of Arts, overseeing a programme that stimulates debate about architecture and its intersection with the arts. She curated *Sensing Spaces: Architecture Reimagined* and *Inside Heatherwick Studio*, which toured east Asia for the British Council in 2015–16. Goodwin was awarded a RIBA Honorary Fellowship in 2016.

WAYNE HEMINGWAY Co-founder of the successful fashion brand Red or Dead, Wayne Hemingway MBE is now a partner in HemingwayDesign, which specialises in affordable housing and social design, including the acclaimed recreation of Dreamland Margate. HemingwayDesign's public festivals, annual celebrations of British creativity, have become acclaimed parts of the cultural calendar.

WILL HUDSON Innovation director at the HudsonBec Group. This group of companies, which is aimed at enabling creativity to thrive, includes media company It's Nice That, creative agency Anyways and creative resource Lecture in Progress.

MANDI KEIGHRAN Australian writer and editor specialising in design and travel, currently based in London. She has worked on a wide range of publications including as editor of Australia's leading architecture and design title *Indesign*, as design editor for *Icon* magazine and as deputy editor for *N by Norwegian*, the award-winning inflight magazine for Norwegian Air.

DAVID KESTER Co-founder of the Design Thinkers Academy and runs strategy studio DK&A. A former CEO of both the UK Design Council and D&AD, David moderates the Dutch design conference *What Design Can Do*. In 2016, he initiated and chaired their design challenge with the United Nations High Commissioner For Refugees (UNHCR) in support of urban refugees.

ANNIINA KOIVU Head of Theory of the MA programmes at the University of Art and Design Lausanne (Ecal) and editor-in-chief of *Interwoven* magazine. She also works as an independent design writer, researcher and curator.

MATEO KRIES Director of the Vitra Design Museum and co-founder of the Berlin-based festival Designmai. His publications include books about Le Corbusier and Mies van der Rohe, as well as about the social, political and theoretical aspects of design and architecture. In 2010 he published *Total Design – Die Inflation moderner Gestaltung*, a critical examination of the contemporary perception of design.

BEATRICE LEANZA Beijing-based curator and critic, Beatrice Leanza was the creative director of Beijing Design Week between 2012 and 2016 and now heads its overseas program. She is co-founder of the research project *Across Chinese Cities*, featured at the 2014 and 2016 Venice Architecture Biennale, and is a member of the advisory board of Design Trust in Hong Kong.

STEVEN LEARNER Founder and creative director of Collective Design, an international design fair based in New York. Learner has worked in the worlds of art and design for more than twenty years as an architect and interior designer, including at his award-winning firm, Steven Learner Studio.

KIERAN LONG Director of ArkDes, the national museum of architecture and design in Stockholm, Sweden. In his twenty-year career he has been working as a journalist and critic, as an educator and broadcaster and, most recently, as a curator in the fields of architecture and design.

SIMONA MASCHI Co-founder and leader of the Copenhagen Institute of Interaction Design (CIID). Believing that design can have a real impact on people's lives and on the planet, she leads a team that encompasses a world renowned education institution, a cutting-edge research group, an award-winning consultancy and an ambitious incubator platform.

BERNARD MCCOY Founding partner at MA! and editor-in-chief of *Design Is Human* – a publication about creative knowledge, the design economy and culture. Based in Atlanta, Georgia, MA! organises the Atlanta Design Festival, MA! Architecture Tour and the Design Economy Expo.

ALEX MILTON Academic, author, curator, professor and designer. Head of the School of Design at the National College of Art and Design, he was the Programme Director of Irish Design 2015, a government initiative that sought to increase the awareness, understanding and use of design in Irish society and industry, and develop a national design strategy.

QUENTIN NEWARK Graphic designer and founder of the studio Atelier Works. Clients include the London School of Economics, the City of Naples, the Houses of Parliament, the People's Liberation Army, Quentin Blake, Camden Council, Tate and the Royal Mail. His book *What is Graphic Design?* was translated into twelve languages, and sold from Beijing to Berkeley.

UGOCHUKWU-SMOOTH C. NZEWI Artist, art historian and curator of African art at the Cleveland Museum of Art. He has curated internationally at major venues including the 2014 Dak'Art Biennale and the 2016–17 Shanghai Biennale. Nzewi's writing has appeared in academic journals, art magazines and edited volumes, including *African Arts*, *World Art*, *Critical Interventions*, *Nka*, *Kunstforum*, *Studio* and *Art Basel Miami Beach* magazine.

PAPA OMOTAYO Creative director of MOE+ artARCHITECTURE and founder of A Whitespace Creative Agency (AWCA). As an architect, artist and film-maker, he seeks to define a pragmatic African modernity through collaboration with contemporary artists and strives to find new possibilities for architecture and visual narratives in Nigeria.

DIANE PERNET Along with pioneering the advent of fashion blogging via her blog 'A Shaded View on Fashion' in 2005, celebrated fashion writer Diane Pernet is also credited with spearheading the fashion film genre, launching *A Shaded View on Fashion Film* (ASVOFF) in 2008. Pernet is in the Business of Fashion (BoF) Hall of Fame.

PHILIPP RODE Executive director of Cities and Associate Professorial Research Fellow at the London School of Economics and Political Science (LSE). The focus of his work is on institutional structures and governance capacities of cities and on sustainable urban development, transport and mobility.

INGEBORG DE ROODE Curator of industrial design at the Stedelijk Museum Amsterdam since 2001. She organized many exhibitions such as *Marcel Wanders*, *Pinned Up*, *Living in the Amsterdam School* and, together with Jeanette Bisschops, *Solution or Utopia? Design for Refugees*. She is currently working on an exhibition about Ettore Sottsass.

NICOLAS ROOPE Cross-disciplinary designer, artist and entrepreneur who has been lucky enough to grow up in the digital era, when ideas can spread like wildfire and the chance exists to connect to communities through their passions like never before. He is co-founder of Plumen, Poke and Hulger & Antirom.

CATHARINE ROSSI Design historian at Kingston University. Her research interests include socially and politically engaged design, craft and nightclubs. Her publications include *Crafting Design in Italy: from Postwar to Postmodernism* (2015). She is currently co-curating an exhibition on nightclubs and design for Vitra Design Museum (2018).

JANA SCHOLZE Design curator, critic and academic. She is Associate Professor at the Kingston School of Art and a Fellow at the Victoria and Albert Museum, where she previously worked as a curator responsible for exhibitions such as *What is Luxury?*. Her most recent publication is a monograph about the designers Edward Barber and Jay Osgerby.

LIBBY SELLERS Design historian, consultant and writer. Before establishing a commercial gallery to support critical and conceptual design, she worked as a curator at the Design Museum for seven years. She is currently completing her third book – a focus on women in design from the last two centuries.

EMILIA TERRAGNI Working as a publisher at Phaidon Press, Emilia Terragni runs the architecture and design department, working with the world's most creative architects and designers, and producing beautifully illustrated books, treasured worldwide for their outstanding content and award-winning production.

BEN TERRETT Group design director at the Co-op and partner of Public Digital. He has won various industry awards including the Design Museum's Designs of The Year and a D&AD Black Pencil. Ben is also a Governor of University of the Arts London (UAL), a member of the HS2 Design Panel and an advisor to the London Design Festival.

ABRAHAM THOMAS The Fleur and Charles Bresler Curator-in-Charge of the Renwick Gallery in Washington, DC, part of the Smithsonian American Art Museum. Previously, he was Curator of Designs at the Victoria and Albert Museum, and Director of Sir John Soane's Museum. He has curated numerous exhibitions, and lectured extensively on modern and contemporary craft, architecture and design.

KAREN VERSCHOOREN Contemporary art curator based in Belgium. As Head of Exhibitions for STUK Arts Centre, Leuven, she is responsible for a series of solo exhibitions and ARTEFACT: an exhibition and festival on contemporary visual arts, current events and societal challenges. She previously curated for Z33, House for Contemporary Art in Hasselt.

NATHALIE WEADICK Curator of art, architecture and spatial practice based in Dublin. She is director of the Irish Architecture Foundation, an organisation committed to communicating the culture of architecture and urbanism to the public.

MATT WEBB Technologist and investor with R/GA Ventures. In 2017 he ran its first London-based start-up accelerator. Previously Matt was CEO and co-founder of BERG, the renowned design studio with work acquired by New York's Museum of Modern Art. He is co-author of *Mind Hacks* (2004) and is currently based in London.

MICHA WEIDMANN Creative director and founder of Micha Weidmann Studio which is based in London since 2001. He works with creators of high-end products to build their brands as well as consults galleries on their exhibitions, publications and online presence. His creative approach is based on his background in Swiss typography and his art direction defined by his work with a broad range of luxury brands.

JANE WITHERS Design consultant, curator and writer. Her studio works with cultural and commercial clients to shape design-led strategies, programmes and exhibitions that bring innovative thinking to address social, cultural and commercial challenges. She has curated exhibitions and events at the Victoria and Albert Museum and Royal Academy of Arts among many others.

PHILIP MICHAEL WOLFSON His studio experiments with fine art and functional design. Its purpose is to examine the way in which we inhabit and interact with our surroundings across the fields of sculpture and installation, experimental design, interactivity, dance and film.

ACKNOWLEDGEMENTS

This catalogue was published in conjunction
with the exhibition Beazley Designs of the Year
2017 at the Design Museum, 18 October 2017
to 28 January 2018.

Curator: Glenn Adamson
Curatorial Assistant: Eleanor Watson
Curatorial Research Assistants: Elena Tamosiunaite
and Tiffany Leung
Exhibitions Project Manager: Claire Corrin
Exhibitions Coordinator: Cleo Stringer
Senior Technician: Stuart Robertson
Exhibition Design: Carmody Groarke
Exhibition Graphic Design: Micha Weidmann Studio

The Design Museum would like to thank all
nominators and nominees who have helped
deliver this year's exhibition.

of Hong Kong: p.59; Ecoalf: p.85; Espen Grønli: p.43; Forensic Architecture: p.81 (t,b); fuseproject: p.143; Grainne Hassett: p.35 (t,b); Gustavo García Villa/NAAFI: p.107; Haraldur Jónasson/karlssonwilker: p.119 (b); Hélène Binet: p.49; HONDA: p.157; IC4DESIGN: p.99; IKEA: p.149; Iwan Baan: p.45; James Morris: p.37; Labadie van Tour: p.135; Leon Chew pp.172–3; Local Motors: p.163; Marcel Sydney: p.125; Marek Z. Jeziorek/Google Inc.: p.63; Mathias Voelzke: p.147; Michael Oswell: p.103; MIT/Christophe Guberan/Steelcase: p.75; MIT Senseable City Lab: p.159; Nathan Smith/Sandy Smith: p.105; Neil Bedford: p.91; Nicklas Dennermalm: p.133; Nike: p.93; OTHR: p.67; Paolo Pellegrin: p.101 (t,b); Paul Vastert: p.129; People's Architecture Office/Gao Tianxia: p.47; Piaggio Fast Forward: p.155; Picturelibrary/Alamy Stock Photo: p.71; Real Review: p.113 (t,b); S27/Fred Moseley: p.57; Scewo: p.165; Seabubbles: p.167; Sergio Del Rio: p.139; Smörgåsbord Studios: p.121 (t,b); Spin: p.117; Teresa Kroeger/FilmMagic/ Getty: p.95; Transport Accident Commission: p.65; Unicode Emoji/Google Inc.: p.77; Wolfgang Tillmans: p.109; Yang Chaoying: p.39

the Design Museum
224–238 Kensington High Street
London W8 6AG

designmuseum.org

First published in 2017
© 2017 the Design Museum

ISBN 978 1 8720 0537 9

the Design Museum
Publishing Manager: Mark Cortes Favis
Picture Researcher: Anabel Navarro Llorens
Editorial Assistant: Giulia Morale
Design: Micha Weidmann Studio

The publishing team would like to thank Simon
Coppock, Jessica Read and Jason Elphick for their
invaluable contributions. Many colleagues at the
Design Museum have supported the publication
of this catalogue and thanks go to them all.

Printed in the UK by Generation Press